From the Valley of Bronze Camels

D0732459

POETS ON POETRY

Derek Pollard, Series Editor
Donald Hall, Founding Editor

TITLES IN THE SERIES
Major Jackson, *A Beat Beyond*, edited by Amor Kohli
Jane Miller, *From the Valley of Bronze Camels*
Tony Hoagland, *The Underground Poetry Metro Transportation System for Souls*
Philip Metres, *The Sound of Listening*
Julie Carr, *Someone Shot My Book*
Claudia Keelan, *Ecstatic Émigré*
Rigoberto Gonzalez, *Pivotal Voices, Era of Transition*
Garrett Hongo, *The Mirror Diary*
Marianne Boruch, *The Little Death of Self*
Yusef Komunyakaa, *Condition Red*
Khaled Mattawa, *How Long Have You Been With Us?*
Aaron Shurin, *The Skin of Meaning*
Kazim Ali, *Resident Alien*
Bruce Bond, *Immanent Distance*
Joyelle McSweeney, *The Necropastoral*
David Baker, *Show Me Your Environment*
Marilyn Hacker, *Unauthorized Voices*
Annie Finch, *The Body of Poetry*

ALSO AVAILABLE, BOOKS BY
Elizabeth Alexander, Meena Alexander, A. R. Ammons, John Ashbery, Robert
Bly, Philip Booth, Marianne Boruch, Hayden Carruth, Amy Clampitt, Alfred
Corn, Douglas Crase, Robert Creeley, Donald Davie, Thomas M. Disch, Ed Dorn,
Martín Espada, Tess Gallagher, Sandra M. Gilbert, Dana Gioia, Linda Gregerson,
Allen Grossman, Thom Gunn, Rachel Hadas, John Haines, Donald Hall, Joy
Harjo, Robert Hayden, Edward Hirsch, Daniel Hoffman, Jonathan Holden,
John Hollander, Paul Hoover, Andrew Hudgins, T. R. Hummer, Laura (Riding)
Jackson, Josephine Jacobsen, Mark Jarman, Lawrence Joseph, Galway Kinnell,
Kenneth Koch, John Koethe, Yusef Komunyakaa, Marilyn Krysl, Maxine Kumin,
Martin Lammon (editor), Philip Larkin, David Lehman, Philip Levine, Larry
Levis, John Logan, William Logan, David Mason, William Matthews, William
Meredith, Jane Miller, David Mura, Carol Muske, Alice Notley, Geoffrey O'Brien,
Gregory Orr, Alicia Suskin Ostriker, Ron Padgett, Marge Piercy, Grace Schulman,
Anne Sexton, Karl Shapiro, Reginald Shepherd, Charles Simic, William Stafford,
Anne Stevenson, Cole Swenson, May Swenson, James Tate, Richard Tillinghast,
C. K. Williams, Alan Williamson, David Wojahn, Charles Wright, James Wright,
John Yau, and Stephen Yenser

For a complete list of titles, please see www.press.umich.edu

From the Valley of Bronze Camels

A Primer, Some Lectures,
& A Boondoggle on Poetry

JANE MILLER

University of Michigan Press
Ann Arbor

Copyright © 2022 by Jane Miller
All rights reserved

For questions or permissions, please contact um.press.perms@umich.edu

Published in the United States of America by the
University of Michigan Press
Manufactured in the United States of America
Printed on acid-free paper
First published July 2022

A CIP catalog record for this book is available from the British Library.

Library of Congress Cataloging-in-Publication Data

Names: Miller, Jane, 1949- author.
Title: From the valley of bronze camels : a primer, some lectures, & a boondoggle on poetry /
    Jane Miller.
Description: Ann Arbor : University of Michigan Press, 2022. | Series: Poets on poetry
Identifiers: LCCN 2022008886 (print) | LCCN 2022008887 (ebook) | ISBN 9780472075423 (hardcover)
    | ISBN 9780472055425 (paperback) | ISBN 9780472220298 (ebook)
Subjects: LCSH: Poetry—History and criticism. | Poetics. | Identity politics in literature. |
    Surrealism (Literature) | Poetry—Authorship. | BISAC: LITERARY COLLECTIONS / Essays |
    LITERARY CRITICISM / Poetry
Classification: LCC PS3563.I4116 M44 2022 (print) | LCC PS3563.I4116 (ebook) |
    DDC 808.1—dc23/eng/20220429
LC record available at https://lccn.loc.gov/2022008886
LC ebook record available at https://lccn.loc.gov/2022008887

Cover art and acknowledgments

Paul Klee, 1879–1940
With Two Dromedaries and 1 Donkey, 1914–1919

Watercolor and gouache over graphite on yellow-toned paper

Image: 9⁹⁄₁₆ × 8⁷⁄₁₆ in. (24.3 × 21.4 cm)
Sheet: 9⁹⁄₁₆ × 8.76 in. (24.3 × 21.4 cm)
Mount: 12⅛ × 9⅜ in. (30.8 × 23.8 cm)
Framed: 24¾ × 22¾ × 1 in. (62.9 × 57.8 × 2.5 cm)
Bernard and Cola Heiden Collection, Eskenazi Museum of Art, University of Indiana,
Bloomington
2000.141

Photo Credit: Eskenazi Museum of Art / Kevin Montague

"Of Mere Being" from OPUS POSTHUMOUS: POEMS, PLAYS, PROSE by Wallace Stevens,
copyright © 1989 by Holly Stevens. Copyright © 1957 by Elsie Stevens and Holly Stevens,
copyright renewed 1985 by Holly Stevens. Used by permission of Alfred A. Knopf, an imprint of
the Knopf Doubleday Publishing Group, a division of Penguin Random House LLC. All rights
reserved.

"May I Ask a Question?" was delivered at the Community of Writers, Olympic Valley, California,
June 25, 2019, at the request of Brenda Hillman.

OF MERE BEING

The palm at the end of the mind,
Beyond the last thought, rises
In the bronze decor.

A gold-feathered bird
Sings in the palm, without human meaning,
Without human feeling, a foreign song.

You know then that it is not the reason
That makes us happy or unhappy.
The bird sings. Its feathers shine.

The palm stands on the edge of space.
The wind moves slowly in the branches.
The bird's fire-fangled feathers dangle down.

Wallace Stevens

Contents

May I Ask a Question?   1

I Love You, a Sob Story (w/ music)   20

Youthful Amours   43

Figs & Fiddlesticks & Politics   59

Javelina Stink. What I Dare Not Say about Poetry   87

Tie Up Your Dinghy & Help Me   115

Fantasia on Paul Klee in Tunisia   138

May I Ask a Question?

1. How Big Is the Bull?

The Japanese poet Masaoka Noboru took for his pen name the word Shiki, meaning cuckoo, because the cuckoo, he learned, is a bird who sings until it bleeds, or so it is said, and that was actually Shiki's fate—he died of tuberculosis. Shiki only lived a brief thirty-five years. He slept poorly as a young man and began coughing up blood. In his twenties, he had to abandon his beloved baseball playing. He'd been a left-handed pitcher and catcher, and after the diagnosis of TB, was one of the first to popularize the sport in Japan by way of writing poems and stories about the sport, such that—for you fans out there—he was inducted into the Japanese Baseball Hall of Fame before he died. Shiki lived during times of great social and cultural upheaval; in fact, he probably is the one person responsible for saving haiku in Japanese culture, and then for other cultures as well. For example, the form has become very popular in English.

My favorite haiku is not set on a grassy diamond. It's a watery scene and it came to mind as I walked through the saguaro desert near my home, up Sweetwater Trail in the Tucson Mountains, part of the Saguaro National Park and quite beautiful. The stricken desert often inspires visions of water. Unusually, as it happens, it had rained heavily overnight, a steady winter rain, different from the rare, thunderous, sweeping summer monsoons. And the steady rain brought out the exotic perfume of the creosote bush. The odor—a distinct, strong musk from the coating on its leaves—is, for native Arizonans, euphoric, with its memory of wind, darkness, and moisture in the air before and after rain. The scent is probably pine, citrus, and camphor. And the Spanish for it is *hediondilla*, loosely translated, "little stinker." Which I guess is one endearing way of describing a haiku.

Here is Shiki's poem, from a man who had the saddest face until he smiled.

With a bull on board
a boat crosses the river
through the evening rain

This is a translation of Burton Watson's, and it raises so many questions, which I'll ask of you, but let me recite it again because it's so beautiful: "With a bull on board / a boat crosses the river / through the evening rain."

"With a bull on board"—how large is the bull? is it black or white? is it black and white? Does it have horns, is it in an open boat, is the boat like a raft, how large is the boat? I have "a" picture, of course I have a picture, we all do by now. I picture a flatboat. And actually, I have a person with a long pole, an older person, maybe a woman, I can't tell because of the oversized blue plastic raincoat, a stooped person whose glasses have fallen into the river and so is having an especially difficult time getting this bull to the other side. But I digress; let me get back to asking you questions: How wide is the river, is this a trip that's going to be half an hour? Is this an all-day or overnight affair? And how heavily is it raining? Is it a mist, a downpour? Is there thunder, lightning? Is it cold, therefore the rain is terribly chilling, or is it a warm night and therefore the rain is welcome? And what is the story of this bull that is crossing the river, is it to meet its destiny to die on the other bank, or to be sold, or is the bull simply on a magical journey that is somehow a metaphor? And is this fairly common, I mean, are boats full of bulls crossing rivers everywhere, were we to look in the direction of the current or upstream? These provocative, charming, and important questions get asked about the life of the bull, the river, the boat, and of course—not more importantly, but as importantly—your relationship to those questions.

2. Is Anything Central?

A great haiku enthralls with its brief description; it *embodies*, in the most physical, immediate way, real stuff such as chilly weather, ticklish laughter, steeping tea, oily rags, sunburn—activity we *feel* in our noses, throats, eyes, and sometimes in our hearts and minds, and sometimes in our souls. But what is description—the heartblood of a poem—*for* in poetry? Are images, as the Romantics showed us, to reinforce a notion of what is beautiful and true? Is our ability to feel the material world with our senses connected to our feelings for other humans, as Jorie Graham suggests?:

> I don't think you can actually be human if you don't know you have a body. You can't have compassion, which is a physical experience at its root. You can't imagine an other, let alone the point of view of an other. You can't have a moral vocabulary in other words.

Are sensorial effects to support an argument, to entertain, or as Graham states, to speak to our very existence? These are questions that are part of the prewriting of a poem for those of us who write poetry. Asking a question peppers the ground, is a visceral experience, and, almost like a sneeze, it instinctively will cause a response in the reader. And a poem also prompts a reader to do the asking, not simply the responding. Anyone engaged with a poem has to wonder, who is speaking, who gets to describe? In fact, our current crisis in subjectivity has to do with this question. Notions of authenticity and of appropriation come into play, especially during this era of identity politics in the arts. Graham goes on to ask, as she puts it, the truly anxious question: "The truly anxious question . . . concerns how singular we are, or remain, or should remain, in relation to our communal predicament . . . This question underpins every other question."

Let's look at someone who used a question directly inside a poem to think about what is central about art and life while there was still doubt about those things, and not that long ago; who steers through a labyrinth of symbols and images in such a way that he literally changed what we ask. You will hear the fourth wall come down immediately, in the opening of a poem written fifty years ago, as John Ashbery inquires as to what really is "The one thing that can save America":

Is anything central?
Orchards flung out on the land,
Urban forests, rustic plantations, knee-high hills?
Are place names central?
Elm Grove, Adcock Corner, Story Book Farm?

The rather hokey speaker in Ashbery's poem will jump around from cities to towers to orchards so swiftly that we come to realize, I believe, that the questions themselves are central. Ashbery opened a very self-conscious, fraught space in our art. He adopts a persona that slowly, slowly reveals a postmodern brave new world, a real advance on confessional poetry, which posited a private one. A "self" guides us to contemplate, via the opening question, centrality, hierarchy, subjectivity, meaning, and perspective as subjects for poetry.

The next generation of writers has added to the inquiry, as to whether anything ought to be considered central, the inquiry: What else but the fate of the earth could possibly be central? That is, is an ethical sensibility central? A leading question like Ashbery's prevents any complacent, lyrical reverie the reader might be expecting in which to relax. You're part of the inquisition.

Another way of including you in the inquisition is to ask, Do you know Layli Long Soldier's book WHEREAS? Here is an excerpt:

> WHEREAS I tire . . . Both of words and word-play, hunching over dictionaries. Tire of referencing terms such as *tire*, of understanding weary, weakened, exhausted, reduced in strength from labor. Bored. In Lakota, tire is okita which means to be tired. Should I mention I'm bored. Yet under the entry for okita I find the term wayuh'anhica, meaning to play out to exhaust a horse by not knowing how properly to handle it. Am I okita or do I wayuh'anhica?

In any language, an inquiry to oneself can be an inquiry to others: Friends, are you just tired or are you seriously mishandling a horse?

3. What Is Love?

You, gentle reader, were likely the last thing on Anne Carson's mind as she delivered one of the most intense breakup scenes in contemporary literature deep into her long poem, "The Glass Essay," which scene, after razor-sharp details, earns a trite, universal question. How does that work in a poem and not come off as a cliché? My sense is that, if you go deep enough into your own emotion, you get to ask anything of anyone, and of the universe itself. Here's her excerpt:

The last time I saw Law was a black night in September.
Autumn had begun,

my knees were cold inside my clothes.
A chill fragment of moon rose.
He stood in my living room and spoke

without looking at me. Not enough spin on it,
he said of our five years of love.

. . .

I don't want to be sexual with you, he said. Everything gets crazy.
But now he was looking at me.
Yes, I said as I began to remove my clothes.

Everything gets crazy. When nude
I turned my back because he likes the back.
He moved onto me.

Everything I know about love and its necessities
I learned in that one moment
when I found myself

thrusting my little burning red backside like a baboon
at a man who no longer cherished me.
There was no area of my mind

not appalled by this action, no part of my body
that could have done otherwise.
But to talk of mind and body begs the question.

Later, in the section "Liberty," Carson risks the Big Trite One, asking not her lover but herself, and by extension, you:

What is love?

Let me ask you, since you are listening: could you say?

4. Do You Want Me to Write a Poem?

The use of a question is the most succinct of constraints. In a prolonged instant, its function in literature is to open, to free; with one formal effect, the listener, the reader, is confronted with an infinity of directions. The question slows things down as we consider, for example, Anne Carson's lament, "What is love?" Slows us, as with desire, to feel and explore, as opposed to the unreal speed of violence, of pornographic speech, of the political catchphrase. In a poem, we reach a threshold when we reach a question. Here, we have choice, time, freedom, emotion, and subterranean, dreamy activity. It is a very full, primordial, adult moment.

The questions we ask ourselves in prewriting, in this postmodern era, have become part of the poem: questions of process, ethics, politics, history, and even whether one is worthy of the name writer, or ought to be selling hats instead, a noble vocation certainly, and yet probably not ours. Although wasn't it the legendary German filmmaker Fassbinder who said, "I'd rather be a streetsweeper in Mexico than a filmmaker in Germany"?

If you are in America and if you are writing poems, you know this a very self-conscious process. Here's how one poet, Chelsey Minnis, has responded. And as you might guess, she questions herself along the way. Here are excerpts from "Greatness":

I don't try to seem very intelligent anymore.
I am beyond such effects.
Like a false limb full of stolen pearls.
Do you want me to write a poem?
Then hold my flask.

. . .

It's just a poem, not a platter of brains.
So don't give me any lucky breaks.
Is it our fault no one fawns on us?
Let's not get forced into the mirrored casket of greatness.
It's easier to write this than to write nothing....

Minnis's super-realism, her brand of exaggerating with entertaining similes, does not hide the fact that she is leading an inquisition into meaning, identity, and the function of the artist in our time.

It is never too soon for an artist to ask herself what the function of art is. I used to think that the function of art was the transformation of sorrow; and later in life I came to agree that the function of art, as William Blake suggests, is to have us "see a world in a grain of sand, and a heaven in a wild flower," that is to say, the function of art is the transformation of consciousness. In our early poem drafts, after the first thrilling, utterly free bathos of material flung onto the page, we are continuously asking ourselves—unconsciously, self-consciously, or naturally—about the depth of thinking in the poem. Our encounter with language is shrouded in inquiry and shifting responses. I would say the sharper the inquiry, the more shrouded the answer.

5. How Long Does It Take?

One of the significant ways that artists get to think through their feelings, and tease out possible answers, is to ask enormous questions like Ashbery and Carson, and to encase them in a documentary landscape. Facts move the poem beyond mere cinematic representation, or presentation, into reportage, binding the relationship between art and life. Listen to the acutely stinging opening of poet danez smith's long poem "Short Film":

not an elegy for Trayvon Martin

the rain has come, thus somewhere
a dead thing is being washed away.

This time, they've named it a black boy.
This time, every time, same difference.

What a great, sad thought he is, this dead boy
clutching tight to sweetness.

How long does it take a story to become a legend?
How long before a legend becomes a god or
forgotten?

Ask the river what it was like when it was rain
then ask it who it drowned.

Perhaps there is no more significant influencer than Rilke if we think about archetypal language, whose principal agent is typically symbolism, which transports us from danez's world of documentation to representation, where angels come, in Stephen Mitchell's translation of the *Duino Elegies*, "and bend you as if trying to create you, / and break you open, out of who you are." Rilke's subject is nothing less than the development of soul in a fraught world. Listen to the writer Nicole Krauss, in an extended passage on legendary history, describe how Rilke came to open his elegies with an overwhelming question:

> . . . Rilke forced himself to work every day, then reeled, weightless, through the streets of Paris, then shut himself in his rooms again to hone the vibrating instrument of his poetry with more solitude, more work. He marveled at the pious dedication of Cézanne, who refused to take a day off from his labors even to attend his mother's funeral. Between 1906 and 1908, Rilke wrote the two volumes of *New Poems* that, despite the nine books that preceded it, mark his emergence as a Great Poet. . . . But he wasn't happy; his real task, he felt, remained undone. Even relationships with others were a distraction. Two more years passed in which Rilke wrote almost nothing.

> Next, he is alone in a Castle, a stony fortress perched on a bluff above the Adriatic, not far from Trieste, where he had gone to visit his friend and patron. He gingerly lowers himself into his "divinely ordained solitude," like a swimmer into freezing water. And there he waits. For despite his hair-shirt regimen of daily work, poems have always arrived to Rilke suddenly, in urgent bursts, like visitations. Then one day, as the story

goes, while marching around on the stormy cliffs puzzling over how to answer a thorny business letter, a voice rings through the gale. Rilke, in awe, takes out his notebook and transcribes what he's heard, and that night it becomes the opening lines of the first of the *Duino Elegies*, and it is a question: *Who, if I cried out, would hear me among the angelic / orders?*

Before we relegate Rilke to the distant galaxy of the early twentieth century, let's remember that he wrote a line that, while not posed as a question, raised more questions than any other half-line of poetry, perhaps in the history of verse, at the end of "Archaic Torso of Apollo": "You must change your life."

6. I'm Nobody! Who are you?

The larger the question, the greater the possibility for all of poetry's equipment to be implicated in the investigation, among the most obvious: description, paradox, intimacy, identity, and mystery. The elusive poet Emily Dickinson seems to be very fond of the question, and makes use, in almost as small a space as the question itself, of all the markers. Here is most of her poem number 260:

I'm Nobody! Who are you?
Are you – Nobody – too?
Then there's a pair of us!
Don't tell! they'd advertise – you know!

How dreary – to be – Somebody!
How public – like a Frog –

This is funny, but it's also profound in its inquiry about the private versus public self. And how about when that frog comes in? Charming, but don't let her lull you. She's using the question "Who are you?" as her main philosophical engine. After an announcement that she's Nobody— with her capital "N," there's some agency there, some existence. She's asking you to consider her opinion about what happens when we are pigeonholed, named, seen, judged. Dickinson, it would appear, is the first of the paparazzi's enemies: How dreary to be "public – like a Frog."

Seemingly far from Dickinson's metaphysics is another poet who charms us, Frank O'Hara. His breezy yet sophisticated tone is also interested in being and knowing. Listen to a section of "Adieu to Norman, Bonjour to Joan and Jean-Paul":

It is 12:10 in New York and I am wondering
if I will finish this in time to meet Norman for lunch
. . .
I wish I were staying in town and working on my poems
at Joan's studio for a new book by Grove Press
which they will probably not print
but it is good to be several floors up in the dead of night
wondering whether you are any good or not
and the only decision you can make is that you did it

. . .
and Allen is back talking about god a lot
and Peter is back not talking very much
and Joe has a cold and is not coming to Kenneth's
although he is coming to lunch with Norman
I suspect he is making a distinction
well, who isn't

If you're paying attention, you heard two embedded questions: "it is good to be several floors up in the dead of night wondering if you are any good or not" and the last lines, "I suspect he is making a distinction / well, who isn't."

These provide cultural, political, and personal moments for O'Hara all at once, and isn't this what we are asking of poetry, to be as multidimensional as possible, like life itself? O'Hara's poem is all very casual, and nothing if not local, but is about power and universals. As it casually pulls the curtain up on his life, the poem is thinking about us: Who are we and what are we doing?

7. What Is the Sound of One Hand Clapping?

Probably since the baby asked the implicit question, "Mama, where's my breastmilk?" the world has been inundated with inquiries. But in terms of queries about the elements that have altered the art of poetry as we know it on this continent, we know that Native Americans were in the Southwest by 7000 BC, asking questions, and we know that by 2000 BC, the Anasazi and the Hohokam, ancestral Pueblo tribes, began farming corn and hunting meat and chanting questions. We have versions of their ancestral songs, which were often filled with questions not only for themselves, but also for the gods:

The corn grows up. The waters of the dark clouds drop, drop.
The rain descends. The waters from the corn leaves drop, drop.
The rain descends. The waters from the plants drop, drop.
The corn grows up. The waters of the dark mists drop, drop.

Shall I cull this fruit of the great corn-plant?
Shall you break it? Shall I break it?
Shall I break it? Shall you break it?
Shall I? Shall you?

Shall I cull this fruit of the great squash vine?
Shall you pick it up? shall I pick it up?
Shall I pick it up? Shall you pick it up?

The ancient combo of question and repetition is really about communion and participation. Art imitates and investigates life. In the Hebraic tradition, for example, we know that by 1300 BC, the Torah is written and contains the Four Questions, written to celebrate the community's freedom from slavery in Egypt. Four questions are asked at the Passover seder by the youngest, and the questions carry the poetic refrain, "Why is this night different from all other nights?" A Q and A ensues: Why do we dip vegetables in salt water? We learn it's to remember our tears. Why do we eat unleavened bread? To remember our humility. And again, Why is this night different? Why do we eat bitter herbs? We need bitter herbs to remind us of our slavery. And why do we recline? We recline because we are free. Call and response.

It is Hellenic culture that formalizes the use of inquiry in the West. "The Socratic question," as we've come to know it, convinces us, without answering any questions, that, ultimately, we know nothing, setting the stage, in terms of making art, for the emphasis on the asking, with its promise of thoughtful, unanswerable choices and humbling refusals. Socrates asks, Why do you say that? His question probes assumptions; that is, what could we assume instead? The question also probes for evidence; that is, can you give an example? Can you imagine an analogy? He often asked his students, Can you give me the counterargument? What's another way to look at this? He also brought to life questions that probe consequences—what are you implying? And finally, he asks questions about the question: Why ask? Does your question apply to everyday life, or what else might you have rather asked? In terms of lessons for poetry, our subject today, one might very well ask oneself these humbling questions through the various drafts of writing a poem to avoid the very worst habit—that of didacticism.

In Chinese culture, it is Confucius asking the questions, in his *Analects*, a record of conversations between Confucius and his disciples concerning the cultivation of oneself through modesty. It is written that the Master asked:

> Isn't it a pleasure to study and practice what you have learned? Isn't it also great when friends visit from distant places? If one remains not annoyed when he is not understood by people around him, is he not a sage?

The Master also asked: "You, shall I teach you about knowledge? What you know, you know; what you don't know, you don't know. This is knowledge." He also famously said, "Someone who asks the question is a fool for a minute; someone who does not ask the question is a fool for life."

Many cultures' questions are audible throughout literary history. Nordic songs surrounding a loss of God in our modernist, fragmented world; African chants about emancipation, assimilation, and identity; and for another example, the enchanting Japanese koan. The koan refers to an unanswerable question, the most famous one being, "We all know the sound of two hands clapping, what is the sound of one hand clapping?" Many answers have been entertained, none of them terribly important; as it turns out, the koan isn't about an object of consciousness; is not a riddle; is not a meaningless statement; but rather is a situation involving an act in which the question, the object of the question, and the one who is being questioned, become one. One hand clapping.

A question, it seems, the noble, gilded, humble, profane, puzzling, inappropriate, untimely, timely, foolish, piquant, or sublime question, has been an arresting and life-changing form of discourse for a long time, and finds itself, in a poem, in a most intense confrontation.

8. Is There Anything Sadder in the World than a Train Standing in the Rain?

When the writer Paul Auster was in Paris, he met Edmond Jabès, a poet living in exile because he was forced out when Egypt expelled its Jews in 1956. Auster says,

> I met him through a chain of friends, poets in Paris. I remember the most memorable thing, I think, he ever said to me about writing, which I think about almost every day. . . . He said, "Well, you know every writer wants to feel as if he's subversive, that he's changing people's perceptions of things, that he's shaking up the world in some way." Then he said, "The only thing that's really subversive in writing is clarity."

Jabès himself whittled this clarity out of a solid block of questions into a beautiful *Book of Questions*. Through question and echo, he contrived an interrogative discourse. He has no patience for anything but the largest philosophical investigations. In "At the Threshold of the Book," he wrote:

"What is your lot?"
"To open the book."
"Are you in the book?"
"My place is at the threshold."
"What have you tried to learn?"
*"I sometimes stop on the road to the sources and question the signs, the world of
    my ancestors."*
"You examine recaptured words."
"The nights and mornings of the syllables which are mine, yes."

Pablo Neruda also wrote a *Book of Questions* during this period. Writing only months before dying in September 1973, the sixty-nine-year-old poet turned to the interrogative by way of anthropomorphism to confront some basics about existence. He puts an eyewitness through coupleted questions:

Tell me, is the rose naked
or is that her only dress?

Why do trees conceal
the splendor of their roots?

Who hears the regrets
of the thieving automobile?

Is there anything in the world sadder
than a train standing in the rain?

Surely there is nothing more intimate, more pressured, like a crystal with its trajectories and intensity, than a direct inquiry. It creates a barrage of possible responses to consider. Like a sudden door knock, an unexpected kiss, a volcanic eruption, a quiver of sound in silence, poetry's inquiry magically pierces various clichéd metaphors—into the rock of death, the fabric of relationship, the center of power, and of course, it goes to the heart of love. On the last subject, the French linguist Roland Barthes had a burning question to ask: "Someone tells me: This kind of love is not viable. But how can you evaluate viability? Why is the viable a Good Thing? Why is it better to last than to burn?"

No poet understands the relation between intimacy and inquiry, nor feels it burn more, than the Russian Marina Tsvetaeva. In a poetic complaint to the man who left her for another woman, the poet's sarcasm mounts in a list composed of "How?" "How?" "How?" "How?" The poem, "An Attempt at Jealousy," piles on cheap emotional intensity, hiding its vulnerability until a last question, when the stakes shift dramatically as the questioner turns the inquiry on herself:

How is your life with that other one?
Simpler, is it? A stroke of the oars
and a long coastline—
and the memory of me

is soon a drifting island . . .
. . .

How is your life with an ordinary
woman? without the god inside her?
The queen supplanted—

How do you breathe now?
Flinch, waking up?

. . .

Is the breakfast delicious?
(If you get sick, don't blame me!)
How is it, living with a postcard?
You who stood on Sinai.

How's your life with a tourist
on Earth? Her rib (do you love her?)
is it to your liking?

How's life? Do you cough?
Do you hum to drown out the mice in your mind?

How do you live with cheap goods: is the market rising?
How's kissing plaster-dust?

Are you bored with her new body?
How's it going, with an earthly woman,
with no sixth sense?

Are you happy?
No? In a shallow pit—how is your life,
my beloved? Hard as mine
with another man?

9. These Words What Can They Do?

Sometimes a poem's question is so intense, especially at the end of a poem, it must be repeated twice, as in the great Zbigniew Herbert's "Elegy of Fortinbras." Fortinbras, prince of Norway, stunned by the gruesome sight of the entire royal family sprawled dead on the castle floor at the end of Shakespeare's *Hamlet*, moves to take over Denmark. Here is Fortinbras at the opening of his elegy to Hamlet:

Now that we're alone we can talk prince man to man
though you lie on the stairs and see no more than a dead ant
nothing but black sun with broken rays
I could never think of your hands without smiling
and now that they lie on the stone like fallen nests
they are as defenceless as before The end is exactly this
The hands lie apart The sword lies apart The head apart
and the knight's feet in soft slippers

By poem's end, where the man of action speaks directly to the introspective, indecisive, and tragically flawed Prince Hamlet, Zbigniew Herbert rises beyond rhetorical commentary and lyric beauty toward a last couplet with a doubled entreaty:

Adieu prince I have tasks a sewer project
and a decree on prostitutes and beggars
I must also elaborate a better system of prisons
since as you justly said Denmark is a prison
I go to my affairs This night is born
a star named Hamlet We shall never meet
what I shall leave will not be worth a tragedy

It is not for us to greet each other or bid farewell we live on archipelagos
and that water these words what can they do what can they do prince

10. What Rough Beast?

When a different kind of prince, the thirty-six-year-old Federico García Lorca, shouts from Spain in surrealist lines in "Encounter," "Can't you see that I'm bleeding to death?" it's remarkable that he will have only two years to live—he will be shot by Generalissimo Franco's thugs. So, when he shouts, "Can't you see that I'm bleeding to death?" it is neither melodramatic nor maudlin. He is already feeling the repression and domination of Franco's government in his bones. Bones that have already suffered; Lorca is said to have become seriously ill when he was young and unable to walk until he was four. He had flat feet, his left leg was shorter than the other, and he always had a limp and a swaying motion. Lorca, whose full name is Federico del Sagrado Corazón de Jesús García Lorca—Federico of the Sacred Heart of Jesus—I'm not a religious person, but that's a whole lot of nomenclature, which asked a lot of him. Lorca, in my view, is among the classic influencers of American poetry because of the rigor with which he questioned himself, norms of bourgeois behavior, language, and, ultimately, death. Yes, it's natural to ask ourselves about the relationship between a writer's life and art, and then ask ourselves, what is the relationship between my life and my work? After all, poetry is not a report or diagnosis. It is a creative act born of inquiry.

Which brings me to our pop quiz—Can you identify another poet, from around the time Lorca is writing, who used the interrogative in the closing of three major poems at the end of his life, and who had a profound influence on the shift in poetry from the pastoral to the political, which, until recently, remained at odds?

Here's the first:

And what rough beast, its hour come round at last,
Slouches towards Bethlehem to be born?

("The Second Coming")

Or how about this one:

Being so caught up,
So mastered by the brute blood of the air,
Did she put on his knowledge with his power
Before the indifferent beak could let her drop?

("Leda and the Swan")

Finally, the luscious:

O body swayed to music, O brightening glance,
How can we know the dancer from the dance?

("Among Schoolchildren")

Those are William Butler Yeats's interrogative lyrics. The poet catapulted us into modernism, in one of art's greatest pirouettes at the end of the nineteenth century, into the political, inquisitive poetry of the twentieth. His Irish political poems asked implicitly if we could ever go back to pure nature poems, and they now ask, more terrifyingly, whether there is nature to go back to. But wait, don't forget about a more contrarian, more American spin on the subject of the question in art, the question, with its attendant frustrations, its existential gloom and doom, its conundrums, its intimacies. It was Gertrude Stein who hated questions because, she said, everybody already agreed with her!

11. What's in a Name?

It's probably the use of a direct, rhetorical question that has lasted as long as any other in poetry. Do you remember, in Shakespeare, when Juliet says, "Tis but thy name that is my enemy. / What's in a name? that which we call a rose / by any other name would smell as sweet"?

We have endless list poems in English full of questions; the buildup to one big question; the question as a subtle aside—these are all wonderful variants. How about the poems where this form admits no answer, not because it's unknown, nor because the questions themselves are unimportant, but because the answer is obvious. In Langston Hughes's "Harlem," he asks "What Happens to a Dream Deferred?" "Does it stink like rotten meat?" The answers are in the form of other questions: "does it dry up," "fester," "run," until finally:

Or does it explode?

One must always be wondering what the next new poetry consists of. Since we are imaginative people, we must ask ourselves, What can be done with language, and toward what purpose? My favorite contemporary use of the interrogative occurs very simply in Jos Charles's beautiful, medieval-postmodern book, *feeld*, a linguistic tour de force of the political and pastoral. I love when poetry returns to its roots in emotion and rhyme, here highlighted with Charles's brilliant hybrid spelling:

/ did u kno not
a monthe goes bye / a tran i
kno doesn't dye

Jos Charles asks the question without stopping to add the question mark, placing the inquiry in a poetry that Charles refers to as speculative realism. Perhaps it's a form well suited to the interrogative—certainly much speculation accompanies their poignant political query. I wonder, do you hear Charles's rhyming and reasoning, both because of each?

12. Who Would I Show It To?

I want to close with a very short poem, where the question constitutes all of the piece; involves empathy, pain, longing, regret, love, loss, grief—all of life, in a poem by William Merwin, who, in one line, devastates us. The title, "Elegy," sadly provides everything you need know about the narrative; clearly someone has died. The one-liner that follows, in the primal plaint of the question, but with no end mark, is so simple, so authoritative, so heart-wrenching, as to almost not exist:

Who would I show it to

Let us grant Lorca a postscript, speaking from a poem written in New York when he was thirty-one: "Don't ask me any questions. I've seen how things that seek their way find their void instead."

I Love You, a Sob Story (w/ music)

The Chinese lyric poet Li Ch'ing-chao was born under the astrological sign of Pisces. Intensity, experimentation, and spirituality define a Pisces generally, although, as we know, we are ruled by forces greater than any single prophecy. Nevertheless, we can imagine that if you are seventeen, intense, and in love with a twenty-one-year-old boy enthusiastic about art and antiquities, a student in the Imperial Academy, it is not unusual to marry him, and for you and your new husband to write poetry together. Nor would it be odd if you spent most of your time and money collecting scrolls, seals, manuscripts, sculptures, paintings, bronze vessels, and rubbings of inscriptions.

Li's idyll with her husband was short-lived. War intervened with the burning of their home and much of their collection. They escaped with fifteen cartloads of books across the Huai River, but, in time, everything was lost. On a fateful trip to a mayoral post, near the newly established Song capital in the south, her husband suddenly got very sick. She barely made it to his side to watch him die. Almost one thousand years ago, it's a destiny as emotionally wrenching, grievous, and immediate as to have happened yesterday, today, or tomorrow.

Already married almost three decades, Li was barely forty-five when she lost him, my wife's age, coincidentally, and the idea of Valyntina grieving over me feels melancholic and melodramatic. Or, if I should lose her, what words then?

It's always difficult for a reader to be as moved as a bereaved or besotted poet by the way her lover swiftly brushes and pins her hair and slips into a bath, for example, or how her lover's strong hand warms her thigh. The intensity of the exceptionally personal is a force field, as anyone who experiences love knows, in which a reader might resist getting involved. Are these notes "grace notes," which, in music, are considered ornamental? Are these quivering moments the essence or the enemy of poems, particularly in poetry about love lost, lost crossed, or love enjoyed?

Li Ch'ing-chao writes, in "To the Tune 'Everlasting Joy'":

The sun sets in molten gold.
The evening clouds form a jade disk.
Where is he?
Dense white mist envelops the willows.

We don't know her husband, but we know mist is symbolically loaded, even if weather on its own is unsentimental. Briefly, we get thrown out of language into the phenomenon itself, then into the speaker's mind processing it. Metaphor increases the pressure of her great sorrow. It compresses complex feelings with a creative figure that, standing in for the feeling, makes companionable sense. Let's not forget that metaphor is chosen as much for its sound as for its sense, that it creates mood, just as any song's rhythm contextualizes its lyrics and meanings.

Consonants and vowels are the raw materials. Li's painterly, balanced sounds, even in translation, reveal a humanity and warmth in the poem's sad mood. The feeling has come into its sound in English in the wistful "w" especially. In translation, the task to represent music is nearly impossible, but Kenneth Rexroth unfurls the pain in graceful, end-stopped English lines, blunted by "Where is he?" Li Ch'ing-chao's graceful bearing of loss is also in Rexroth's version of "I Smell the Fragrance of Withered Plum Blossoms on my Pillow," where anguish struggles from the throat in the grunting and guttural sound of the vowel "u":

Last night, so very drunk,
I fell asleep in makeup and jewelry
Withered plum blossoms still in my hair.
. . .
I unrolled the kingfisher-green curtain,
Crumpled the fallen petals . . .

This lament from a thousand years ago is light years away, aesthetically, from the Language poetry movement of the late twentieth century, which attempted to correct an assumption that voice is the foundational principle of lyric poetry. Language poems do have what Marjorie Perloff calls a "signature"; absent a "confession," they convey a flow of meanings and contexts with wordplay, gaps, syntactical derangements, and discontinuity. So, where has postmodernism's critique of interiority left the love poem, with its emotions on its speaker's sleeve? Never very far from death, tragedy, and time.

While Language poetry decentered or deleted the speaker of a poem, compositional clots and tensions illustrative of personal events never did disappear. By 2017, Ben Lerner is saying, about post-avant-guardians Maggie Nelson and Claudia Rankine, respectively, "Both *Bluets* and *Don't Let Me Be Lonely* open with a mixture of detachment and emotional intensity that simultaneously evokes and complicates the status of the 'lyric I.'" He continues, "The shift, from the tactical deconstruction of ostensibly natural narrative or lyric unities, to the effort to reconstruct them with a difference, is legible."

The twenty-first century now overflows with a "reconstructed" poetry of identity politics that features historical documentation in lyrical hybrid narratives. Poetry is constantly, it seems, constructing and reconstructing the "lyric I." The ostensibly surrealist poet Odysseas Elytis begins his 1969 poem "Villa Natacha," "I have something incomprehensible to say, / like birdsong in time of war." Elytis, who had been a young lieutenant in the army, later said in an interview "it became necessary for me to proceed toward that spearpoint where life and death cease to be contraries." He continues,

> Fear, the physical fear of war, the material fear of bombs and shells, annihilated in me all aspect of false literature and left naked the meaning of a true need for poetry.

Years later, he wrote to another Greek poet, Kimon Friar, "I believe in the restitution of justice, which I identify with light."

Cathy Park Hong reinscribes the necessity for such personal documentation, calling out attacks on the lyric as "a symptom of the avant-garde's 'delusion of whiteness,'"

> its specious belief that renouncing subject and voice is anti-authoritarian, when in fact such wholesale pronouncements are clueless that the

disenfranchised need such bourgeois niceties like voice to alter conditions forged in history.

If you are a writer, you may find yourself in love and writing a poem that has your sweetheart, your country, or your cause all over it. Moreover, if a tragedy has befallen you, prompting a crisis, is not this exactly where poetry is most necessary? Isn't tragedy private but common? How does that sound?

Bowed, Plucked, Struck

Shangyang Fang, who once wrote in a poem that the loneliest music was a Brahms piano concerto, "like drinking a bowl of Chinese herbs in the dark," sent me the pained song of Liu Yong, the Song poet who lived in a brothel most of his life. Liu Yong's lyrics, like Li Ch'ing-chao's, broke from euphemisms of the boudoir into real sensitivities. In the song, a monk chants from the Heart Sutra under the surface of a mandolin, wooden fish (a wooden bell), banjo, flute, runan (a lute with a fluted neck), pipa (a pear-shaped lute), and zheng (a plucked board zither, basically a rectangular box with strings). The monk's voice seems both primordial and also preprogrammed, in consort with the zheng in particular.

Suddenly another voice enters, a male singer with a wounded ache, heartache, perhaps, judging by its quaver, followed by yet another voice, this one crawling with strange, thin, pinched notes, which Shangyang says is made as if squeezing a man's throat (https://www.youtube.com/watch?v=L8f6NbamNpU).

How obviously expressive music is without words, or without words we understand! To my ear, this piece contains the full range of love's language, its longing, grief, and mystery. Its several voices and old instruments have much in common with postmodern poetry's many registers in one poem—high and low dictions, short and long lines, multisyllabic and one-syllable words, and the glorious lessons of synesthesia, where the senses intermingle. The song reminds me that poetry also can have a nonnarrative, nonlinear structure and still be deeply moving. While narrative's advantage is that every human story, subject to time, is potentially poignant since it ends in death, discrete lyric strands that remain unresolved, or sound discordant, can communicate passionately. They create a context for themselves.

I have a few modern Chinese flutes that I cherish, and after listening to Shangyang's gift of music, I wanted to learn about the older Chinese instruments. During the Tang dynasty, a century before Li Ch'ing-chao is writing her lyrical poems, many of the emperors wrote and composed music themselves. A golden age of exotic instruments produced music braided from many cultures. Many of the old instruments make atonal and screechy noises, primordial sounds, some nearly inaudible, to my American ear. In a wonderful example of synesthesia, they're grouped by *material* into eight sounds, or *bayin*—silk, bamboo, wood, stone, metal, clay, gourd, and skin. The voices of these instruments open a new canal of audial perception for the untutored ear, suggestive of new sounds to represent the *cri de coeur*. Amplified or softened by the material of which they are composed, I hope they inspire us to find equally strange sounds and combinations in our familiar alphabet, which rise up through the instrument of our mouth, throat, and lungs.

Listening with our Western ears to instruments of the ancient East can remind us that music offers a shade of anonymity to words—as if they move through darkness—because it is abstract. It may act like a diaphanous sheet covering our exposed forms. The provocative effect is suggestive of a subtle sensuality, like seeing a lover barely draped in a towel or sheer gown rather than familiarly naked.

Hearing a familiar alphabet anew, in fresh combinations of words, is an honorable goal for the poet. As the sounds fill the space in a poem, strange juxtapositions may return poetry to its ancient voice of augury and awe. Readers may not always understand the meaning of a new word choice and word order, but getting their attention may confirm, beyond reason, that a soul is speaking, perhaps is wounded, angry, or smitten. Isn't that intuitive knowledge, for the reader, a form of love?

Silk

A very intimate poetry might take cues from a zhonghu, whose softly plucked, bowed, or struck silk strings are tuned to a low register. The tone is closer to rain on soft metal than to the higher, scratchier, tangy, glassy pitch of a horsehair bow plying contemporary violin strings made of nylon, steel, or sheep intestine. This is the zhonghu: (https://www.youtube.com/watch?v=1zOccV6fTh8).

Now listen to its transposition into language, what I perceive as a bowing of silk in Li Ch'ing-chao's "Song of Departure," in an achingly soft English translation, again by Rexroth, with variations of the letter "o," spoken with the mouth open:

> . . . Gently I open
> My silk dress and float alone
> On the orchid boat. Who can
> Take a letter beyond the clouds?
> Only the wild geese come back . . .

Maybe you find her poem precious, too delicate for your cosmopolitan ear. Love poetry can be saccharine, like love itself, I suppose. But Rexroth has brought her carefully considered word choices of ten centuries ago, clear note by note, into sensual English without piling up multi-syllables of abstract and intellectual Latinate words. The ideographic nature of the original Chinese, in which a written character symbolizes the idea of a thing without a word or sound, is, put simply, a picture, as in the case of numerals.

Poetry under the influence of the earliest Chinese system of pitches, which ensured that all twelve notes sounded as often as one another in a piece of music, proceeds in parallel lines with little emphasis on enjambment. Early in our last century, Ezra Pound's *Cathay* presented translated "versions" of this flat plane of Chinese poetry using Ernest Fenollosa's scholarly notes. But Pound's versions were, as he puts it in *Cathay's* subtitle, "*for the most part* [my italics] from the Chinese of Rihaki" (aka Li Po, Li Bai, Li Bo, etc.). Most of his errors, where there were errors, tended to exoticize the flat tones by depending on English's internal rhyme, assonance, and consonance, raising and lowering pitches, often altering meaning. Compounded by Pound not realizing Fenollosa's glosses were not translations per se, it may yet be true, as Mary Caws wrote in her *Surprised in Translation*, "Pound makes a slightly wrong meaning into a completely right feeling."

Pound's opening of "The Beautiful Toilet" by Mei Sheng inserts linking verbs and conjunctions to provide momentum and heighten the scene:

Blue, blue is the grass about the river
And the willows have overfilled the close garden.
And within, the mistress, in the midmost of her youth,
White, white of face, hesitates, passing the door.

While he ultimately circumnavigated the Chinese pentatonic scale, adding various instrumental parts of speech in tension, it seems to have allowed him to cross the interpreting brain barrier into magic and mood to hear our alphabet and syntax anew. The rest, one might say, is the American Imagist movement.

I feel living scenes in Pound's and Rexroth's translation work, Imagism's pictorial precision. I'm afraid that, in substituting timbres of vowels and consonants for the original pitch and measure of frequency to suggest tone in their translations, something is lost forever. But I am heartened to have an otherwise undecipherable essence from long ago and far away.

Listen again to the stringed zheng, heard earlier accompanying a monk's flat chant, now solo, in scrapes like a twangy, rattling banjo (https://www.youtube.com/watch?v=ujzMHLac404).

Perhaps you hear this plucking in "Seaside," a Charles Wright translation of a Eugenio Montale poem. It has similarly nasal, bright, and low vibrations to my ear. The agitation is darkly sexy. Nasal "n"s build at the end, the soft "p"s pop, the "r"s flutter nearly every line, until the several "l"s of the last line roll to a stop at the letter "k," which is made with no quaver:

The air rattles, the darkness is torn to shreds,
and the shadow you threw along the fragile
palisade curls up. Too late in the day

if you want to be yourself? The rat plops
from the palm, the lightning is on the fuse,
is on the long, long lashes of your look

The clanging, squeezed, and pinched sounds give texture and odd companionship to mellifluous notes. They encourage a particularly bold, animal sensuality.

In another example of his commitment to Montale's unusual clanging diction, inflections of language, and rhythm, Charles Wright chooses "j," "g," and "-ing," for a tiny, high-pitched orchestra of sound, before "The Storm" resolves, literally, into a disappearance, in this fragment:

> . . . *the tearing crash, the jangling sistrums, the rustle*
> *of tambourines in the dark ditch of the night,*
> *the tramp, scrape, jump of the fandango . . . and overhead*
> *some gesture that blindly is groping . . .*
>   *as when*
> *turning around, and, sweeping clear your forehead*
> *of its cloud of hair,*
>
> *you waved to me—and entered the dark.*

I also hear another silk-stringed instrument, the higher pitches and short plucks of the bold pipa, in "tramp, scrape, jump of the fandango . . ." (https://www.youtube.com/watch?v=N4j4B15Iq7g). The Tang dynasty poet Bai Juyi has described the sound:

> The bold strings rattled like splatters of sudden rain. . . . Chattering and pattering, pattering and chattering. As pearls, large and small, fell on a jade plate.

Lamentation sounds very different in Paul Celan's post-lyrical poetry. John Felstiner has to deliver a German of gaunt grief-shards into English, where Li's translator, Rexroth, has found the soft-spoken adjectives "withered" and "fallen" in the Chinese originals, and Charles Wright has given us Montale's clanging and squeezing music. Celan, to me, resides in the skeletal tones of another classic string instrument, the jinghu, which releases squeaky, thin, nasal notes, a nearly human keening or far-off geese squawking, flying on a cloudy day. The silken strings seem to screech against metal. The bowed jinghu can also chirp, neigh, or bleat. Made of sandalwood, it's referred to as the barbarian's violin, originating with nomads. Its silk strings intone an anxiety quietly—minimally, like Celan—because of a small sound box. Snakeskin covers the front. The back is open. It's typically bowed from the back, that is, from behind, the silk (https://www.youtube.com/watch?v=RbCpFTSBpJA).

The jinghu seems to be playing nearby, even though behind me. It has a nervous, high-pitched melancholy, as though someone I care for deeply is leaving. These feelings are set in a grim, near-silent landscape in Celan's "Homecoming." Tragedy has crushed words into a new vocabulary of traces and glints, metal filings. And yet he is one of our greatest love poets. His short-lined stanzas seem to emanate from the jinghu's small sound box:

Snowfall, denser and denser,
dove-coloured as yesterday,
snowfall, as if even now you were sleeping.
White, stacked into distance.
Above it, endless,
the sleigh track of the lost.

Below, hidden,
presses up
what so hurts the eyes,
hill upon hill,
invisible.

On each,
fetched home into its today,
and I slipped away into dumbness:
wooden, a post.

There: a feeling,
. . .

It is only in the last stanza that we find "There: a feeling," which continues, "blown across by the ice wind." Celan strains, in his solitude, to reach an other, a "thou," as he said in his extraordinary speech "The Meridian": "A poem is making toward encounter, homecoming." After the Holocaust, in which both his parents were murdered, he said, "There remained in the midst of the losses this one thing: language." He wanted a dialogue between one era and another, one language and another, you and me, poet and reader. His music, because it is soul-speaking, is excruciatingly touching to me. Paul Celan's poems represent the nearly pure sound of love, unmediated by extra syllables or slack, didactic rhetoric. Reader, if it is in your destiny to love and be loved, destiny will leave one of you in hell. But if you are Paul Celan, everything and everyone has gone, and you leap after them into language, as into water. If you are Li Ch'ing-chao, you carry your boxes from one rental to another until your landlord steals the last of your ink stones. "Frailer than yellow chrysanthemums," but still a poet.

Skin

Beating on things to produce a sound, and through that sound to express various emotions, is said to have begun in the early stages of human development, where people stomped on the ground or beat their own bodies. Drums developed in ancient China can be flat, worn around the waist, shaped as a barrel, or set in a frame. My favorite is the bangu, a Chinese frame drum that, when struck by one or two small bamboo sticks, creates a sharp, dry sound essential to the aesthetics of Chinese opera. The bangu player is often conductor of the orchestra, setting the mood by timing and volume. The player strikes a small area called the drum heart. It reminds me of certain sharp, pointed moments in poetry, signifying urgency (https://sites.google.com/site/chinesemusicleahpatek/technique/instruments/bangu).

Osip Mandelstam advises us, "At the very deepest stages of language there were no concepts, only directions, fears and longings, only needs and apprehensions." This deep expression sounds like skin struck, in the ending of a translation of a poem by another Russian, Marina Tsvetaeva, very lightly, as you'll hear, with an eyelash:

Where does this tenderness come from?
And what will I do with it? Young
stranger, poet, wandering through town,
you and your eyelashes—longer than anyone's.

We don't learn the stranger's tender acts, but we hear the incautious willingness at the heart of the poet, who is doomed to lose everything eventually, because time is the true subject here. Momentary pleasures cannot compare to the knowledge that the world, over time, is not kind. It makes the speaker's openness to an encounter daring, even in translation, echoed in the intimate sound of short vowels and subtle rhymes, of snatches and echoes, as time itself is composed, and, struck minute by minute, passes. Urgency must be as raw in language as it is on drummed skin, on fluttered face or breast. I feel as close to Tsvetaeva as skin on skin because of her impetuous nature, the suddenness with which she telescopes a moment down to the smallest possible image, "eyelashes." My face draws very, very close to hers. In keeping the "you" and "your eyelashes" equivalent in size and import by the word "and," translators Ilya Kaminsky and Jean Valentine offer us the surprise and intimacy that must be in the original fragment. Tsvetaeva once said, "There cannot be too much of lyric because lyric itself is too much."

Bamboo

The voice of a love poem, with its specific lyric register, first person, and general quality of intimacy, may sometimes recall the nearly human sound of an acoustic instrument in an open-air setting. My dizi, for example, a flute made from southern Chinese white bamboo, lighter in weight than purple or violet, is especially responsive outside, may twitter, play cheerfully, or whisper in very human tones. It hangs in the air before disappearing. A penetrating timbre comes from a tissue-like shaving of membrane trembling over an extra hole. Creating fine wrinkles in its application is an art form in itself.

The dizi master Yu Xin Fa invented the contemporary koudi, the smallest Chinese flute, taking its shape from prehistoric instruments made of bird bone. It achieves the dizi's similarly remote pitch, a high, quivering skylark sound that carries far into space, which the listener hears as if from a long time ago

(https://www.youtube.com/watch?v=m2NqEqVKQW4).

Something as mournful as this tiny flute happens to love poetry when memory, that is, when distant time, enters the frame.

This morning I woke
in a bamboo bed with paper curtains.

I have no words for my weary sorrow,
no fine poetic thoughts.
The sandalwood incense smoke is stale,
the jade burner is cold.
I feel as if I were filled with quivering water.

It is morning for Li Ch'ing-chao, and the paper curtains, stale smoke, and extinguished burner hurt her. Time revises the very place and face of romance differently for every poet. Li Ch'ing-chao's "quivering water" is more impressionistic and symbolic than Czeslaw Milosz's metonymic images in this excerpt from his "Elegy to N.N.":

You could have run over the small waves of the Baltic
and past the fields of Denmark, past a beech wood
could have turned toward the ocean, and there, very soon
Labrador, white at this season.
. . .

you had a path straight through the wilderness
over blue-black, melting waters, with tracks of deer and caribou
as far as the Sierras and abandoned gold mines

Milosz winds our way from Eastern Europe's beech woods to California's manzanita, big oaks, and eucalyptus to trace the route by which a woman from his past might find him. While Milosz's images aren't metaphoric, the simple descriptors "small," "white," "blue-black," remind me of Ch'ing-chao's "yellow," "west," "eastern," in "T'zu 18":

. . . I drink wine by the eastern fence in the yellow dusk.
Now a dark fragrance fills
My sleeves and makes me spin.
The bamboo blinds sway in the west wind.
And I am even thinner than a yellow flower.

As the speaker drinks wine, end-stopped lines represent years marked off, the passing of time. Short vowels hurry by, memories carried by wind. Though worlds and ages apart, Milosz's and Li Ch'ing-chao's poems are each convincingly site-specific. They both prepare us for the eventual self-effacement of the speaker/poet by the impermanence of the place we once thought immutable. We learn of intimacy ground down by history. "I too accepted but what was possible," Milosz writes. While not defeat exactly, the words share the sorrowful flute's knowledge. The flute calls and calls and no one comes. In Milosz's poem, the end is sobering:

No, it was not because it was too far
you failed to visit me that day or night.
From year to year it grows in us until it takes hold,
I understood it as you did: indifference.

These poets share a consciousness about the past that Roland Barthes, thinking about photography in *Camera Lucida*, named a "having-been-here," as opposed to a "being-there." This unusual tense is love poetry's magical space, crowded with ardor, rage, forgiveness, hurt, and wistfulness, but it provides for metaphysical and spiritual revelation, too. Having-been-here: a grammar in which a first action has been completed, and yet "here." It does not express nostalgia, or what we would call derogatorily, "a waxing poetic"; rather, the poet moves rapidly through feeling into thought.

Intensely voiced poetry is at the edgy place of what Judith Butler names the "constructed world" and its "interpreting" speaker. If, as Butler suggests, "subjectivity . . . is conceived of as something both constructed and constructing," emotions guide the performance of subjectivity. Love comes out of nowhere to ravish and quite possibly ravage us—how closely they sound! Maybe we come to poems about intimate relationship for the truth of Barthes's intimating our "having-been-here."

Metal

The secret life of sound in art offers what facial expression, body language, voice volume, and silence offer in life—measured contact. Poets search various speeds and sounds for the intent of the poem, its spirit, by getting in touch with their breathing ("spiritus," Latin for "breath"). Plosives, for example, which stop airflow, seize the poem, as if against material and mortal limits, and often work to prevent lines from overheating. They ring out in a brief announcement and then are shut down, like metallic hanging bells, flat gongs, or finger cymbals trapped by the hand. Some bells sound particularly intimate and delicate, but a bianzhong, while known as a holy bell, rings hollow and cold, housed in bronze (https://www.youtube.com/watch?v=zhcCSeRj2PU). The anguish of loss, as chilling and hallowed as these metal bells, is nearly impossible to repeat in translation. But I admire Merwin's version of Federico García Lorca's great "Gacela of Unforeseen Love." Many plosives of the original remain, with their subtle, contracted pain in the breath. A door blows open into a "garden of my agony":

No one understood the perfume
of the dark magnolia of your belly.
No one knew you tormented
a hummingbird of love between your teeth.

A thousand Persian ponies fell asleep
in the moonlight plaza of your forehead,
while through four nights, I embraced
your waist, enemy of the snow.

Between plaster and jasmine, your glance
was a pale branch of seeds.
I sought in my heart to give you
the ivory letters that say always,

Always, always: garden of my agony,
your body elusive always,
the blood of your veins is in my mouth,
Your mouth already lightness for my death.

The words choke on the "k," "d," and "g" of "dark," "gaze," and "magnolia" in three sensuous stanzas in the past tense, followed by the lover's departure into the future in the last stanza. We arrive as if having raced through a phantasmagoric night to meet someone: "the blood of your veins is in my mouth." "Crushed" and "torture," with "t" and "c," make a Roman candle firework "crack" sound or a dull strike of metal. The poem itself thinks in paradoxes and oppositions—"love"/"death," "jasmine"/"plaster." It's vibrating, expanding, and shrinking, until we, too, are instruments of Lorca's passion.

It is in love poetry such as Lorca's that a tug of forces is extravagantly performed, yet the verses themselves are compact and tightly wound. The private love poem remains a site from which neither rhetoricians, philosophers, nor Language poets have been able to eliminate agency. And because the personal always seeps into the social—to begin with, we are breathing, literally "expressing," outward—the poem of passion also finds a natural home in an age of documentary poetics. Passions extend beyond their intended borders.

To house your extravagant feelings, can you find a language of austerity inside yourself, such as is heard in a distant bronze ringing? If art is cold, because it is not alive, it's made lively by proxy. In Lorca's case, the future is as cold and resonant as ancient bronze, a painful and contracted sound, nearly always death itself. Is he our greatest love poet because of that intimacy?

Wood

The sound of wood knocked, chopped, or walked upon is probably the opposite of a hollow sound. Wood is warm, alive, aging, and instruments made from it retain the spirit of a living tree. It may be the closest equivalent to the lifeblood of words in love poetry. Warmth in a poem is not something spoken about, but rather enacted in sensorial activity. It makes me think of Dante Alighieri, who employs all the senses in his fluid grammar, humanizing the alphabet.

Dante begins a legendary journey in a metaphoric woods. In Seamus Heaney's version, sounds and sense resolve and re-configure—"in a thick of thickets, in a wood so dense"—rather than succeed one another. The lines roll back and forth, listing forward, achieving Dante's motility. At one point in his beautiful essay "Conversation on Dante," Russian poet Osip Mandelstam describes the "workout" in reading Dante: "One has to run across the whole width of the river, jammed with mobile Chinese junks sailing in various directions. Its route cannot be reconstructed by interrogating the boatmen: they will not tell how and why we were leaping from junk to junk."

I can nearly hear the Florentine walking the dirt path because of the naturalness of his voice, which strides along earnestly, even in translation:

In the middle of the journey of our life
I found myself astray in a dark wood
where the straight road had been lost sight of.
How hard it is to say what it was like
in the thick of thickets, in a wood so dense
and gnarled
the very thought of it renews my panic.

Ancient wooden clappers, which sound of muffled, trotting horses on packed marl, are percussive instruments that share Dante's steady stride. Worn around the wrist like the handbells of a belly dancer, clappers are slightly larger than the hands that play them. The cushioned sound rolls back and forth between a slap and a clap from hand to hand (https://www.youtube.com/watch?v=mHztae9dz0c).

One ancient wood percussive instrument is carved in the shape of a tiger with a serrated back, played by hitting a whisk across it. The slaps remind me that I sometimes say to a classroom of bruised students, "I'm sorry your mother beat you with a wooden spoon," meaning, we've all got our pain, but the problem is how to present emotion so that the reader feels as much—though not the same—as the writer. It is a good start if we don't censor our thoughts but shape them. A poem isn't an "emoting" into a diary. In Dante, I always feel the unfolding poem reflects the writer's newest knowledge, enfolding what came before, stanza over stanza, as hand over hand. It seamlessly becomes something else.

While Dante's poem opens in the metaphoric woods, watery music carries his convertible images along on a diaphanous barge. The waters are rough, gentle, restless, warm, or still, and, at the bottom of hell, frozen. There, Dante treads on the heads of sinners in a frozen lake, some supine with only their heads above the ice, such that their tears freeze in their eyes. "Suffering crosses the organs of sense," Mandelstam says of Dante's synesthesia: "their eyes, which were only a little moist, / now gush out through their lid lips." A "labial eye," Mandelstam terms the hybrid, akin to thinking of instruments in terms of the material of which they are made. It is a reminder that the greatest instrument, our own voice, synesthetically *feels* sound in the mouth.

By the end of *Paradiso*, the music of the journey resolves in the mellifluous sounds at the vulnerable front of the mouth, especially with the heavenly "l" of "l'amor che move il sole e l'altre stelle," preserved in C. H. Sisson's lovely version:

> But already my desire and my will
> Were being turned like a wheel, all at one speed
> By the love which moves the sun and the other stars.

It's a music worthy of its centuries of study by scholars, poets, and students. As if on a psychedelic drug, we travel with a speaker who is vibrating through a huge range of stimuli. But it's always along a steady tercet, beating a humane and gentle passage, as if played on wood, a still-alive, gentler material than the stone or bronze of earlier ages. Dante made language sound new, not only by his choosing vernacular Italian rather than Latin, but also by making an alphabet sound like a natural material.

Clay

The tolling of a single, disquieting syllable is never very far from the beloved's gorgeous, gleaming body in Allen Ginsberg's sexually explicit elegy for Neal Cassady:

> . . . mouth my tongue touched once or twice all ash
> bony cheeks soft on my belly are cinder, ash
> earlobes and eyelids, youthful cock-tip, curly pubis
> breast warmth, man palm, high school thigh,
> baseball bicept arm, asshole anneal'd to
>   silken skin all ashes, all ashes again

We hear Ginsberg's funereal end note, "ash . . . ash . . . all ashes again," even as he's trying to breathe life into Neal's body by naming the shapes. Yet the torso remains piecemeal, as in the work of the sculptor Gaudier-Brzeska, who left the body "unfinished," with the tool marks still on the human form. Even though death has broken the body, Ginsberg caresses Neal with a chant, a droned, stretched refrain from ancient religious ritual. If man is made from clay in the miraculous birth theme, this poem makes him fleshy before he burns down to ash. The repetitions in the poem suggest the cycling of life, the infusion of breath by spirit. The ocarina, or xun, a ceramic wind instrument of fired clay, has Ginsberg's bare tone of a willow whistle, or an animal mourning its young. It is as if, in the firing of the ocarina, something of the original suppleness remains of the mud from which we are mythologically made. An unbearable sweetness hovers over its disconsolate sound

(https://www.youtube.com/watch?v=Coi0Lgq7sRo).

Many of the acoustic ageless instruments of China have this nearly unbearable, fatalistic register. The sound makes me weep, not only for Neal's life, abbreviated at forty-one, but for Life.

Stone

Just now, when I saw you naked again,
I thought the same words: rose-rock, rock-rose . . .
Rose, trying, working, to show itself,
forming, folding over,
unimaginable connections, unseen, shining edges,
Rose-rock, unformed, flesh beginning, crystal by crystal,
clear pink breasts and darker, crystalline nipples,
rose-rock, rose-quartz, roses, roses, roses,
exacting roses from the body,
and the even darker, accurate, rose of sex—

It appears that love poetry was hard for Elizabeth Bishop to keep unwritten. "Vague Poem" unleashes the most passionate, nearly Gertrude Steinian signs in *Edgar Allen Poe and the Juke-box: Uncollected Poems, Drafts, and Fragments*, unearthed by editor Alice Quinn in 2007. The excerpt is a rare glimpse of Bishop in an intimate, sexy setting, rather than at a gas station, by a river, over breakfast, et al. She's indulging in the rhythmic seduction of lyricism's most sensual vowel ("o"), pronounced with the mouth in an open circle, and in sensual, vibratory consonants (f, l, v, m, r) quivering from the front of the mouth, a tip of tongue exposed (as in our famous English word, "love"). I find an equivalent tone, a light tinkling, in the bianqing, ancient jade chimes:

(https://www.youtube.com/watch?v=LEa4BlnufqY).

A love poem can't flourish without air; Bishop probably never intended anybody to see the scribble. Reader, do you blush? Is it too much, too soft, too many delicate "o"s, without death and disaster to offset the erotic notes? As light as the jade chime's tinkle? But the agent of the poem is the associative and cold "rose-rock." And darkness ("darker ... darker") is there, no? It recalls James Wright's poem "Sappho":

> ... Love is a cliff,
> A clear, cold curve of stone, mottled by stars,
> smirched by the morning, carved by the dark sea
> Till stars and dawn and waves can slash no more,
> Till the rock's heart is found and shaped again.

The rose quartz in Bishop's poem is virtually as hard as jade, which, in the form of jadeite, is the toughest known mineral, stronger than steel. Both hard, pink stones are associated with the heart chakra and, as symbols of purity, are reminders to hold nothing back, lest there be self-censorship, in the expression of passion.

Significantly, jade is not a single cut crystal like gold or ruby, but a cluster of microcrystals, invisible lattices of flat surfaces with innumerable faces. It would seem that its purity is enhanced, rather than corrupted or compromised, by multiplicity. Mined and carved in China since the Neolithic Age, over 6,500 years ago, jade has a distinguished history as an object of decoration and ceremony. Used practically, as a rest for a calligraphy brush or a mouthpiece for an opium pipe, jade would ensure a long, pure life by breathing through it, or by writing with its vibration inside. The mineral is known as a symbol of benevolence for its luster, and of integrity because it may be broken but not twisted. Chimes made of jade are two thousand years old, reverberating from much farther away, a place as old as love itself. While pink jade and pink quartz share attributes of color and density, Bishop unceremoniously chose the much more common element to represent the extraordinary female form.

Gourd

Caravaggio's *Still Life with Fruit on a Stone Ledge* features two bottle gourds, enormous serpentine fruits that probably reached Europe at a very early date from Africa. Like many grapes and melons, the flowering plants contain seeds, and probably exist in Caravaggio's early seventeenth-century painting for their cylindrical, bulbous shape. The painting interests me as an extraordinary paradigm for poetry because, painted from life, it includes representations of disease, insect damage, and normal physical defects. Poetry's passionate diction has got to be as intense and sometimes as gross as the specimens that fill the artist's stone table and fill out the frame—gourds, pomegranates, melon, grapes, and figs in various stages of beauty and decay.

A gourd itself makes a brash, bold sound when its so-called "wind chest" is attached to pipes with finger holes, a tone like a tangy, droning kazoo or bagpipe. Pointedly, the player must breathe through her nose while pushing air from her cheeks, a breathing-without-stopping, analogous to a poet breathing life into a poem by continuous attention (https://www.youtube.com/watch?v=OJApHaTvHZ0).

This hulusi instrument has a youthful, exuberant blare, without the cool metal of a trumpet, but with a trumpet's surety. Its assertiveness seems to be in a category with Caravaggio's hot, fleshy, boy-man narrative, *Amor Vincit Omnia* (Virgil's "Love conquers all"), a painting starring his lover, Cecco. The subject's young face, toned body, and adolescent energy break out of chiaroscuro and wings. The shading creates definition and aggressively spotlights. Love and beauty, it would seem, emerge against dark, ancient, and immutable laws, where time and death famously exert their will. Caravaggio adores a severe range of contrast—very bright and very dark; stylistically, fruit and nude are interchangeable. The painting is a wonderful reminder of extremes to which a poem may go, and which, in the affective setting of love poetry, may flaunt a desperate, exaggerated frankness. A poem needn't clang, but as it sustains its force, it suggests a feeling of being constantly in a reader's face as a continuous outpouring, with the goal of leaving its audience, paradoxically, "breathless."

Frank Stanford's tragic poem "Freedom, Revolt and Love" also features youthful love in a drama that is both dark and light. The poem's sweet, doomed lovers don't know as much as the poet knows, judging by the audacious title. While Stanford's pair are a stock invention, the real world hasn't been kind to them. Except for love. Here is most of the poem, before they die:

They caught them.
They were sitting at a table in the kitchen.
It was early.
They had on bathrobes.
They were drinking coffee and smiling.
. . .
They saw them through the window.
She thought of them stepping out of a bath
And him wrapping cloth around her.
He thought of her walking up in a small white building,
He thought of stones settling into the ground.
Then they were gone.
Then they came in through the back.
Her cat ran out.
The house was near the road.
She didn't like the cat going out.
They stayed at the table.
The others were out of breath.
The man and the woman reached across the table.
They were afraid, they smiled.
. . .
She started to get up.
One of them shot her.
She leaned over the table like a schoolgirl doing her lessons.
She thought about being beside him, being asleep.
They took her long grey socks
Put them over the barrel of a rifle
And shot him.
He went back in his chair, holding himself.
She told him hers didn't hurt much,
Like in the fall when everything you touch
Makes a spark.
He thought about her getting up in the dark
Wrapping a quilt around herself
And standing in the doorway.

It's a classic movie scene, maybe of the *Bonnie and Clyde* variety, with pathos and tragedy, romance and reality, sentimentality and death all caught up together. It's a set piece, and civilization will go on outside, like the cat. That's the future in the poem, and it catapults the reader like a slingshot. The lovers are ruined, a real sob story you pretend you saw coming. Feelings are not literally expressed. The intimacy is gestural. "They took her long grey socks / Put them over the barrel of a rifle / And shot him." It's a suspiciously straight-up narrative, except that it lacks momentum. It is alive in discrete shots and interiority, with the action, despite its abject seriousness, almost beside the point. The poem is a tableau about life, not death.

It's Valentine's Day as I write, so forgive a little hyperbole in my saying that some lines in here just "kill me," such that when I get to "The man and the woman reached across the table. / They were afraid, they smiled," you know that they are smiling at each other for no reason but that they are in love and trouble. I think Frank Stanford is heartbroken for all the world's ill-fated. In the end, I hear maybe a slow strike of twisted silk or a trail across the strings of the poem.

Love in poems such as Stanford's, lacking irony, humor, political rhetoric, or any postmodern slippages, risks mawkishness, and probably isn't for everyone. Terrence Des Pres, author of *The Survivor*, a tormented study of survival in the death camps of the Holocaust, felt that love alone, love apart from the world, could never be an answer to life, contrary to its representation in Western art in Plato's cave, where comfort is real, but encourages cowardice. Stanford's genius lies in putting Death at the table, tapping soundlessly, steadily, drinking coffee, taking its time. Maybe the "kids" are poor—because I'm involved now, I'm politicizing the poem, as all poems invite social readings—young lovers distant from family, maybe they've done something crazy and, as the first line reveals, "they caught them." Or maybe they did nothing but be wild and easy to blame. I hear a radio playing in the background, maybe the bright sound of the hulusi, falling between a southern banjo and clarinet, but made from a natural shell resonant of earth.

Thinking about these desperados puts me in mind of a much older voice, that of a troubadour poet, Bernart, from the twelfth century. Bernart would not be having breakfast with his love, with trouble brewing. His trouble is constant and present. He's waiting in vain for his beloved, resorting, in one stanza, to two exclamations, much repetition, and the unabashed self-proclamation that he's a "poor yearning wretch":

Mercy is gone, that is sure,
And I never received any of it,
For she who should have the most mercy has none,
And where else should I seek it? Oh! How difficult it is for a person who sees her
To imagine that she would allow to die this poor yearning wretch,
And would not help the man
Who can have no help but her!

Always at risk: to the lover, the situation may be tragic, but to the reader it sounds pathetic. Bernart's long fourth line gets especially whiny, like the hulusi played continuously with quavering vibrato. An ache of music draws breath in a plaint of words. The courtly lover's situation sounds particularly vulnerable to amusing the cynics and confirming the pessimists, as it typically shuts down any hope of either an intimate evening or a full relationship.

The courtly poet expresses a platonic, noble love, in which one accepts the independence of the other and acts honorably to be worthy of attention. This suggests my relation to you, dear Reader. And while I would seldom recommend abstinence, humiliation, or fanciful exaltation, the courtly lover's desire for connection seems virtuous. A call for a response. Was sexual satisfaction possible? It may have been beside the point; the point of interest becomes the process by which one engages in a series of tests to prove one's ardor. In that regard, this has been my pleasure.

Youthful Amours

1.

A bog in Black Moshannon State Park provides a habitat for orchids not common anywhere else in the state of Pennsylvania, including the small, purple-fringed orchid, whose spectacular petals resemble butterflies. Orchids should never be removed from the wild, as they will probably die if transplanted. Winter transplanting, cutting out a frozen sod, is especially difficult, or so I'd heard. I had no intention of stealing any. In my late adolescence, I'd often drive to the park and lie around by myself, even in cold weather, and read poetry. To be frank, I thought of myself, romantically, as a frozen sod of an orchid. Not that I imagined I was beautiful, or valuable. Simply that I wanted to be left alone.

I often heard Canada warblers because the park sits high up on the Alleghany Front. European settlers had clear-cut the vast old-growth white pines and eastern hemlocks, but the forest was replanted in the 1930s. In the bog, I saw my first great blue heron, which was white, rare, and probably strayed north from Florida, a bird I'd confuse later in Northern California with the great egret, whose legs are black. It may seem a trifle to know the difference. But minutia matters to a poet, even to a poet who doesn't know yet that she is one, but who has noticed that nature and language both reckoned with likenesses and differences, the differences of similar species, and the shades of meaning of similar nouns or verbs.

How alike were the feelings, "I love you" and "I'm in love with you"? That was a big question among my friends. Was there a difference of degree, or kind? If phrases appearing similar were different, maybe different phrases could be similar. I remember thinking hard about a phrase in literature class, "evening is spread out against the sky," which Eliot had equated with "a patient etherized upon a table." It seemed as far away as two images could be and be relational. Amazing.

The heron symbolizes stillness and tranquility, two qualities I lacked, and sought in the woods. A heron, as it happens, may be more suitable than the purple-fringed orchid as a symbol for my young Taurus self, not because my bearing was especially regal, but because I modeled myself after the heron's ability to survive in a bog's poor soil and to wade through its mud without getting, as the cliché has it, "bogged down." I wanted to move swiftly out of the old clichés of angst and innocence. I wondered if words could lead me out of that self. Also wondered how some overused words attained archetypal status, like moon, sun, sea, and, for a while, stone, door, and bridge, while other symbolic words lost their connections to us. Slowly, I began to write poems.

My mother often regaled us with Yiddish sayings, and I wasn't sure if her expressions were worn out, or tribal and significant. "Go shit in the ocean" sounded comic, mean, and stinging, and still calls up crazy images to me. Mostly chastising, a few of her idioms crackled with originality, as in one for the stepfather she despised, roughly translated: He should be transformed into a chandelier, to hang by day and to burn by night.

Winters in Pennsylvania were very dark. I read many, many poetry books in the university library, alphabetically, up to Neruda, at which point I began to read vertically, that is, everything of his, in mostly awful translations, until fortunately, one night I found W. S. Merwin's 1969 translation of *Twenty Love Poems and A Song of Despair*, still the Chilean's most popular book. Published in 1924, it launched an unknown poet into the stratosphere of the literary arts. Pablo Neruda was barely nineteen. It was his second book. I was overwhelmed by its sensuality.

Stephen Dobyns, in his forward to a 1993 edition, tells the story of Neruda taking questions after a poetry reading in the 1960s, confessing he didn't have a particular poem, number twenty, with him when asked to read it. At which point, four hundred people stood up and recited it to him!

Even in a translation, Merwin's, such romantic, heartbreaking pleasure:

Tonight I can write the saddest lines.

Write, for example, "The night is starry and the stars are blue and shiver in the distance."

The night wind revolves in the sky and sings.

. . .

Tonight I can write the saddest lines. To think that I do not have her. To feel that I have lost her.

To hear the immense night, still more immense without her. And the verse falls to the soul like dew to the pasture.

What does it matter that my love could not keep her. The night is starry and she is not with me.

This is all. In the distance someone is singing. In the distance.

I've broken the excerpt, in a poem I've heard disparagingly referred to as a poem for beginners, on a line I love: "In the distance someone is singing" as the fractious world goes on. It always reminds me of the Auden poem about Brueghel's painting of Icarus, in which

The expensive delicate ship
That must have seen
Something amazing, a boy falling out of the sky,
Had somewhere to get to and sailed calmly on.

Years later, after I'd met W. S. Merwin, he asked to stay with me in Tucson to be near his dying friend, the painter Bruce McGrew. Merwin chanted every morning and evening from the *Tibetan Book of the Dead* to ease Bruce's consciousness through death into rebirth. The chanting transformed my small study, where my guest slept, into a small cathedral. I've come to believe that rhythms, chanting, and singing, part of the great vibrating of life, are ongoing, and from time to time, whether something amazing happens, or life goes calmly on, poets connect to the energy they feel and transcribe the sounds. I'm not a religious person, but I'm in awe of the universe. Merwin would finish by circling a small copper bowl with a mallet crafted of Himalayan hardwood and a padded surface until it sang. I still hear it, and you can, too.

I lived with Richard, an artist, for most of my twenties. We were a family. Two hippies in search of art and life, not realizing the difference, or more exactly, their relationship (let alone ours). It was an age of "enlighten-ment." A feminist movement and an anti-war movement exploded into the streets and canceled an old world, or so we thought. I took the hallu-cinogenic LSD. The trip lasted two days, and on it I saw I could get out-side of myself and not die.

We lived in Berkeley. I worked at a public radio station and was sent to cover a poetry reading of Judy Grahn's. Afterward, after I rolled up the electrical cords and packed the microphone, I watched, in awe, women slow-dance with each other and kiss. I realized that I probably loved Rich-ard but was not in love. But neither of us had any money, so together we moved north, to cheaper Humboldt County, lived in a redwood forest in a house of redwood, and burned fallen redwoods to stay warm. Richard carved the ones too beautiful to burn. We also grew pot, aromatic hairy-looking buds. It rained and rained. From time to time, I went into Arcata to Jambalaya, a bar where a band played in a spotlit corner. Many soggy (future famous) writers and artists would hunker in from the rainforest to hear a great bass player, a decent guitar player, and a gravelly singer. I remember, in particular, the painter Martin Wong's beautiful, pale hands as he shyly crossed through the crowd. I joined a women's group of paint-ers. We would pose for one another and talk. It is here I started to enjoy life. That is, I culled a few ideas, a start, about living and making art. First idea: practice.

I devoured Merwin's poetry and translations after my encounter with his Neruda poems. Only men published in the big presses. I read into Eliot and far into Stevens. I went back through and read Keats and Shakespeare and many of the other guys again and again. Alternatively, I read wom-en's presses and small magazines. It seemed like two different universes. I fell in love with a woman. I read the European surrealists, the New York School, the Harlem Renaissance writers, the Black Mountain poets, the Russian lyricists, the Eastern European ironists, and Chinese, Japanese, and Imagist poets, mostly to impress her. I loved James Wright. I loved Langston Hughes. I was pissed that Plath and Sexton killed themselves, and Berryman too, that crazy fucker, who I ought to have hated for his loathsome self-absorption and drunken behavior toward women. But I loved him too.

I dared not read Dickinson, although I tried. I felt, with no proof whatsoever, that she was desperate for intimacy and unfulfilled. She frightened me. Her metaphysics and intellect seemed all she had of a disembodied reality. It took years to realize she made her own reality, thank you very much. I wanted her to have had sex! Which is why I preferred Whitman. I was coming into my body power and I wanted to drag everyone with me. I slept with a lot of people. I read and loathed Bishop. I'm not sure why, although I hated that she was closeted.

Richard and I eventually moved to Iowa City to educate ourselves. I met Jorie Graham, Jim Galvin, Joy Harjo, Rita Dove, Brenda Hillman, and others. There were very few schools for studying creative writing, or so it seemed, and the town filled with ingenues. Poets from hamlets and college towns and granite cities. I studied with Carolyn Kizer, Bill Matthews, Marvin Bell, Donald Justice, and Louise Glück. When I'd first made the waiting list for admissions, we caravanned out of California. Richard drove a Volkswagen bug, towing a giant redwood log on a flatbed (he was accepted to a program to study sculpture), and I followed in my old Swedish car with a sheaf of poems and rolled canvases of beginner's oil paintings. I couldn't draw well, but I had a sense of color and composition that helps me now.

We drove straight to Marvin Bell's house and he invited me in to recite my poems. This welcome seemed like a perfectly normal thing to have happen. Next, Sandra MacPherson read them on Monday and I was accepted. I was terrified of Donald Justice and relieved to have avoided him in the selection process. But it was through him that I encountered Lorca, the love of my literary life. One day I read Justice a poem of mine in his office and he said bluntly: too sentimental. Then he read me this:

I want the water reft from its bed,
I want the wind left without valley.

I want the night left without eyes
And my heart without the flower of gold.

And the oxen to speak with great leaves
And the earthworm to perish of shadow.

The poem ends:

But do not illumine your clear nude
Like a black cactus open in the reeds.

Leave me in anguish of dark planets,
but do not show me your cool waist.

That is the opening and closing of "Gacela of the Terrible Presence," in *El Diván del Tamarit*, which Lorca wrote in his last years. *Diván*, from the Arabic, refers to a collection of poems, and *tamarit*, to the country estate in Andalusia, near Granada, where Lorca wrote most of the collection. The lines quiver with sensuality and chilling foreboding. Lorca was very soon ordered murdered by the grotesque tyrant Franco. The titles in the book derive from two Arabic forms, the *gacela* (ghazal) and the *casida* (qasida), which deal respectively with love and death. *Gacelas* traditionally have an erotic component, but Lorca's love poems reveal death and love to be inextricably wound (homonym, "wound.") Lorca hurts.

I found Edwin Honig's *New Versions of DIVAN & Other Writings*, published in 1977, with Lorca's strange, disembodied self-portrait ink drawing on the cover. The poems chanted with urgency, frankness, and premonitions, yet most of it made little narrative sense. This excited and liberated me. Where could a poem go, or more pointedly, where could it not? Lorca was not the first visionary and mysterious sensibility to whom I was exposed. But he allowed me to close the gap between the surreal and real because of his combinatory agility in so many poems, like this simple and dazzling image from "Gacela of the Morning Market": "flash fire in the snow." I decided to contact Edwin Honig about another of his translations, "Gacela of the Dark Death."

It was inexplicably both violent and tranquil: "I want to sleep the sleep of that child / who longed to cut his heart open far out at sea." The language was so basic and primordial, it seemed that Lorca had written in English, or that Edwin Honig himself had written the poems. Intimations of danger infused the intimacy and made long shadows. Honig wrote back asking if I myself was a poet and, if so, might I send him a few poems. Shyly, I did, later to learn that he was not only a translator, playwright, biographer, and poet, but also founding editor of Copper Beech Press, and he wanted to publish my first book. This true story remains a miracle to me. A dusting of Lorca's innocence and experience.

I moved to Vermont because I was running away from a woman. Louise, my teacher and friend, offered to let me stay with John and her. It was Louise, too, who suggested I go down to Goddard College nearby and try to get a job. Jim Nolfi met me by chance on the Northwood path, as I was searching for his office—he was a dean, but he looked as ragged as everyone else—and interviewed me and hired me on the spot. Not because I was qualified, but because many of the undergraduate faculty of poets, artists, and scientists, unbeknownst to me, had quit suddenly on some point of honor that I never fully gleaned.

I invited Adrienne Rich to read her poems in my official role as Undergraduate Program Director (a position that, fortunately—and never quite so perfectly again, in over forty years of teaching—did not involve academic meetings). I don't know why I chose her exactly, except that I knew her essays, and also I thought if I invited a woman, and made mistakes with my hosting duties, she would forgive me. Funny, because Adrienne Rich could be astringent and demanding, although she was kind then, and later. That subzero night, I thought no one would show up for a poetry reading, but over three hundred people packed in for her. The fire marshal could not get the people standing in the aisles to leave. When I introduced her, the ovation literally shook the rafters of the old Haybarn Theatre, built in 1868 by the Martin Family and one of the largest barns in central Vermont.

Rich read in a formal, nearly ritualistic, tone. She read erotic poems and poems of liberation. If no one understood that the personal is political, then that night it became clear. Quickly, her poems broke into extraordinarily intimate terms. Her power against normative, polite behavior was intense. She was alive with subversion and integrity. She read from *Twenty-One Love Poems* and from *Dream of a Common Language*, about to be published. She recited:

If I could let you know—
two women together is a work
nothing in civilization has made simple,
two people together is a work
heroic in its ordinariness

It was a great night, maybe the first night of living alone in which I did not feel lonely. I was twenty-eight, my first book was in production, and I had a job. Eight feet of snow fell the next day and blocked the door, the birch-lined driveway, and the narrow road from my cabin to the rest of civilization. My romantic self hunkered down to work.

2.

A boondoggle is a work that is pointless, but which gives the appearance of having value. My literary inheritances probably mean little to somebody else. But if I write these passages to reaffirm my interdependence with words, perhaps a lost young poet, looking for a sign that her own poetry is of the essence, will be encouraged. This may be a boondoggle, and furthermore, if all art is, in some sense useless, or at any rate, meaningless, it is also a calling. What some people are hearing may be beyond understanding, but also suggestive and connective. In other words, poetry opens time and space, and puts you, as Robert Hass writes, "in possession of other people's experience. The famous formulation of this fact was made by the great Chinese poet Li Po who wrote to a friend, the other of the greatest of the T'ang dynasty poets, Tu Fu: 'Thank you for letting me read your new poems. It was like being alive twice.'"

As I write this brief history of my early literary education, I confess to forgetting a lot. Maybe I read Pound's Chinese versions later, in my thirties or forties, and maybe I read Frank O'Hara later, too.

For certain, I read with wide eyes Strand and Simic's *Another Republic: 17 European and South American Poets* in 1976, which included a constellation of geniuses—Paul Celan, Italo Calvino, Yehuda Amichai, Nicanor Parra, Czeslaw Milosz, Julio Cortázar, incredible! Also incredible: not one woman, a fact which crushed my spirit and my heart while my mind doggedly read the anthology over and over. You could also find the Polish poet Zbigniew Herbert there, unlike anyone I'd ever heard:

FIVE MEN

1.

They take them out in the morning
to the stone courtyard
and put them against the wall

five men
two of them very young
the others middle-aged

nothing more
can be said about them

2.

...

now they lie on the ground
covered up to their eyes with shadow

...

3.

...

so why have I been writing
unimportant poems on flowers

what did the five talk of
the night before the execution

of prophetic dreams
of an escapade in a brothel
of automobile parts
of a sea voyage
of how when he had spades
he ought not to have opened
of how vodka is best
after wine you get a headache
of girls

of fruits
of life

thus one can use in poetry
names of Greek shepherds
one can attempt to catch the color of morning sky
write of love
and also
once again
in dead earnest
offer to the betrayed world
a rose

This stark assassination by firing squad nonetheless affirms a role for the poet, who is destined to see and hear everything, the betrayed world as well as the rose. I slogged through a bog of failed drafts after studying Herbert and, soon after, Czeslaw Milosz, who, with Peter Dale Scott, had translated "Five Men." A few of Robert Hass's translations from Milosz's Polish had begun to appear in small magazines. I was intrigued because my ancestors were from Poland, from the village of Prushnitz, taken over in the first days of September 1939 by the Germans after a devastating battle led by a Colonel Jan Karcz. If my grandparents had not gotten out earlier and made the crossing in steerage to New York, they would have been in hiding or in a death camp. I imagined their village of farmers and tradespeople, along the Węgierka River, to resemble the landscape of Milosz's amazing poem, "Dedication," with its confrontational question:

Here is a valley of shallow Polish rivers. And an immense bridge
Going into white fog. Here is a broken city;
And the wind throws the screams of gulls on your grave
When I am talking with you.

What is poetry which does not save
Nations or people?
A connivance with official lies,
A song of drunkards whose throats will be cut in a moment

The poem is bitter and unsentimental, filled with the guilt of a survivor, as he turns abruptly from violence, from the past. He closes by addressing the war dead with his gift of poetry:

They used to pour millet on graves or poppy seeds
To feed the dead who would come disguised as birds.
I put this book here for you, who once lived
So that you should visit us no more.

International poetry had blood written all over it. It had the same streak of Adrienne Rich's rhetorical determination built into its lyrical/narrative structure. In Marina Tsvetaeva's case, it rose into a lyric so pure and intense, the voice seemed to come from someone alive after a fire. "All Russians are Jews," Tsvetaeva boldly declared, while herself not Jewish, perhaps because they think they are keepers of memory with no place to live in the world. Elaine Feinstein's incredible translations from the Russian of my grandmother Goldie's Odessa, on the Black Sea, broke me with the power of a feeling I didn't yet know existed, the anguish of lost love. I felt as though I'd walked into a mirror with somebody's else's history; so personal is her feeling that it becomes, miraculously and naturally, familiar. In her long masterpiece, "Poem of the End," she writes of the disintegration of her most passionate love affair as the couple walks across Prague, crossing real and metaphoric bridges:

Now we kiss soundlessly, his
lips stiff as
hands are given to queens or
dead people thus

round us the shoving elbows of
ordinary bustle
and strangely irksome rises the
screech of a whistle

howls like a dog screaming
angrier, longer: what

a nightmare strangeness life is
*   at death point*

and that nightmare reached my waist
*   only last night*
and now reaches the stars, it has
*   grown to its true height*

crying silently love love until
*   —Has it gone*
six, shall we go to the cinema?
*   I shout it! Home!*

It's almost too much! Chaotic, yet focused with cinematic precision, as if filmed with a handheld camera inside and outside her head. It seemed she instinctively required jump-cuts like the director Sergei Eisenstein used. Had she seen his work? It made me want to study film, and eventually sent me to the genius Andrei Tarkovsky, whose long takes and slow pacing allowed space for spiritual and metaphysical themes to emerge. He explored faith and death like Ingmar Bergman, but less darkly, or so it appeared, in dramas less self-absorbed, more universal and symbolic.

Even as a mere apprentice to poetry, I learned that art was not an indulgence but a necessity, that it involved thinking at the deepest level of being. As a poet and a Jew and a nascent lesbian, it must have been that the violent world in need of sacrifice and empathy demanded my attention. I needed help. Then I met Olga.

She lifted me in the air when we met and flew me around, a sign of things to come, of travel, of the light-headedness of love. Broumas had recently been selected by Stanley Kunitz as the Yale Younger Poet. I admired the sensuality and feminism of *Beginning with O* and was enthralled by her. It was love quickly, so transforming as to seem, at first, unreal, I suppose like any important discovery. She wrote of our falling for each other in "Landscape with Leaves and Figure":

Passionate Love is Temporary
Insanity the Chinese
say that day

I walked nine miles in the bowl
the hill makes coming round
and round avoiding
the road in
sane I realized a whole
week later at the time
I sank my crepe
soles in the spread
of leaves grass needles
bedding down the path
I took […]

When we moved in together, she introduced me to the complicated, abstract, and passionate poetry of Odysseas Elytis, whom she was translating. He had just won the Nobel Prize in Literature and entrusted her with bringing his work into English. In his acceptance speech in Stockholm, he praised the spiritual reality of art. He spoke of the ineffable's "intervention" in Byzantine icons and of spirit painted in tempura on wood, cast into metals, and carved into marble. He forcefully felt a vibration, a magnetism, from small, stylized marble figures of five thousand years ago—many now housed in the Goulandris Museum of Cycladic Art, in Athens. He wrote of these women of pure white stone, sometimes painted with mineral-based pigments, azurite for blue, cinnabar for red, with arms folded across the front:

> I am thinking here of the manner in which the sculptors of the Cycladic period used their material, to the point of carrying it beyond itself. I am also thinking of the Byzantine icon painters, who succeeded, only by using pure color, to suggest the "divine."

It is just such an intervention in the real, both penetrating and metamorphosing, which has always been, it seems to me, the lofty vocation of poetry.

As one struggles as a writer, one occasionally glimpses someone else's poem that is undefinable but instantly recognizable, transparent, and luminous. Listen to parts of sections III and IV of Elytis's "The Monogram," a love poem for the ages, and especially a love poem for one's twenties, as one's passions flare. How earthen and primordial the images of sea and sky, and yet they are convivial with the surreal, the mystical, and the illusory. It is a love poem not only to a beloved person but to a beloved homeland by a poet forced into exile by military dictators:

It is still early in this world, do you hear me
. . .
It's me, do you hear me
I love you, do you hear me
I hold you and take you and dress you
In Ophelia's white bridal, do you hear me
Where do you leave me, where do you go, and who, do you hear me
. . .
I am not going anywhere, do you hear me
Either neither or together both, do you hear me . . .

From so much winter so much north wind, do you hear me
To pull a flower, only we, do you hear me
In the middle of the sea
From just the wanting of love, do you hear me
Raised a whole island, do you hear
With caves and coves and flowering gullies
Hear, hear
Who speaks of the waters and who cries—hear?
Who looks for the other, who shouts—hear?
It's me who shouts and it's me who cries, do you hear me
I love you, I love you, you hear me

Time, beauty, and nature balance in "a hymn to the visible and the beautiful," as Robert Hass has said of "Famous Night," another Elytis poem from *What I Love*, which begins:

> . . . by the terraces, near the musical complaint of your hand's curve. Near your transparent breasts, the uncovered forests full of violets and vegetables and open palms of moon, far as the sea, the sea you caress, the sea that takes and leaves me leaving in a thousand shells.

What transporting world was this? The world I desired.

For me, metaphor has all the transformative power necessary for psychic survival. It is food and water for the soul. Comparisons, associations, disjunctions, personifications, allusions—a fractional list of poetic proofs of the interrelatedness of the universe. Olga and I spent the end of our twenties together, in love and poetry, before we parted in a malaise of errors. Olga, an accomplished musician as well as translator and poet, taught me much about impassioned language, its roots in ancient epics, lyrics, and pastorals, and even more about silence, openness, and translucence. I learned that the work of poetry is witness and praise. Lyric poetry, in particular, seemed closest to real life, although, paradoxically, it was barely there, whereas life with Olga was kinetic and full. A lyric poem still feels efflorescent and radiant to me, like sea foam cresting and returning to the sea. As Elytis's "birdsong in time of war," poetry is natural and inexplicable.

The halcyon days of passion, of learning, and of youth are, of course, far from peaceful. Rather more like floating in rough winter seas, clinging to the life raft of an idea that is innocent and beautiful. It is said by ancient writers that the mythical bird, the halcyon, breeds in a nest floating at sea on the winter solstice, charming the wind and waves into two weeks of calm in order to give birth. I like to think that I still cling to beauty and that I am nesting, even now, hoping for a next poem. While the bluebird is the symbol of happiness in many cultures, the halcyon, better known as the kingfisher, seems the more perfect poetic bird to represent the idyll that is one's youth, especially because the kingfisher closes its eyes as it dives into water, flying blind.

A startling flash of orange, cyan, and blue erupts when the notoriously shy flyer takes off. While the orange of the kingfisher's breast plumage is the product of tiny pigment granules, the blues of the back, wings, and tail contain no pigments. They're created by an intricate structural arrangement of transparent material, bedazzling in sapphire, cerulean, and ultramarine when light shines on them, and darker cobalt, indigo, and midnight blues when in shade. The bird's appearance is an illusion, a wonder, and a festival. Its beak design is so clever that the Japanese model the front of their bullet trains after it.

All aboard! Valyntina, my love, has just now called me from reminiscence, after a surprising rain in the desert, to see a rainbow, created as light enters clear droplets, slows, and bends them. That is, light separates the drops into wavelengths of color by reflecting off their insides, and when the light finally exits the raindrops, it makes an archway of primary color. I doubt, but some say, that it is God hovering over the water. I'd say, it's wonderful, as one's youthful study is a wonder and, from this distance, not so much about what it means, as what it's for. To get one's attention and to figure out one's intention.

As those years disappear, it is the winter solstice again. The world survives in midst of a deadly pandemic, as horrible a year in its way as 1939, when Odysseas Elytis wrote his love poem "The Monogram" against the agony of time. He made the same passionate appeal in his Nobel Lecture:

> Innumerable secret signs, with which the universe is studded and which constitute so many syllables of an unknown language, urge us to compose words, and with words, phrases whose deciphering puts us at the threshold of the deepest truth.

> In the final analysis, where is truth? In the erosion and death we see around us, or in this propensity to believe that the world is indestructible and eternal?

Because I felt both powerless and indestructible as a young poet, I trusted guides and followed them. I've read that three seagulls flying together are a warning of death, and that sparrows carry the souls of the dead, and ought not to be disturbed. I suppose one must intuit how far to follow.

Figs & Fiddlesticks & Politics

Hubba, hubba, hubba

After the famous couple yielded to the temptation of the snake, ate the fruit, opened their eyes, and discovered they were naked, they looked for cover. It's an old story, Genesis 3:7 to be exact, wherein "they realized that they were naked; so they sewed fig leaves together and made loincloths for themselves." The gigantic leaves are themselves nearly obscene, given the biblical recommendations for prudence and moderation. Though they never needed clothing before, the knowledge of good and evil created a fearful urge in our young pair to hide from each other and protect themselves. The consequences of their rebellion would be disastrous. The rest is religion and politics, involving power, procreation, shame, death, serendipity, relatives, prayers, and gardening. Also poetry.

Judy Grahn's "The Marilyn Monroe Poem" has a different version of good and evil. When I heard Judy Grahn read the poem in my twenties, after an education in long-dead white poets and recently suicidal confessional poets, I was shocked. She belted out a critique that reveled in discourses deliberately feminist, openly lesbian, unabashedly sexual, and brutal:

I have come to claim
Marilyn Monroe's body
for the sake of my own.
dig it up, hand it over,
cram it in this paper sack.
hubba. hubba. hubba.
. . .
Long ago you wanted to write poems;
Be serious, Marilyn

I am going to take you in this paper sack
around the world, and
write on it:—the poems of Marilyn Monroe—
Dedicated to all princes,
the male poets who were so sorry to see you go,
before they had a crack at you.

. . .

Now I shall take them my paper sack
and we shall act out a poem together:
"How would you like to see Marilyn Monroe,
in action, smiling, and without her clothes?"
We shall wait long enough to see them make familiar faces
and then I shall beat them with your skull.
hubba. hubba. hubba. hubba. hubba.
Marilyn, be serious
Today I have come to claim your body for my own.

The poet reclaims Monroe's body from the male gaze, male violence, and male possession. The poem's attack, "I shall beat them with your skull," was the first instance I had heard, in poetry, violence reversed, directed at the male. Grahn challenged the idea of the domination of men over women, a concept immortalized at the Creation, with Adam made first, from the dust of the ground, followed by Eve, from a rib taken out of Adam's side.

Grahn's performative refrain, "hubba, hubba, hubba," became increasingly malevolent and mocking the more she chanted. The poem's lesbian offensive officially liberated me from heteronormative culture. After the event that night, I vowed to read more poems "by women." I hated its designation as a subgenre; it was imperative that it speak, as we say, its truth, on equal terms. Soon I found Adrienne Rich's essays, which she would collect in 1978 in *On Lies, Secrets, and Silence*. In Anne Sexton's honor and memory, Rich listed some of the ways women destroy themselves:

> Self-trivialization is one. Believing the lie that women are not capable of major creations. . . . Being content to produce intellectual or artistic work in which we imitate men. Horizontal hostility—contempt for women is another.

I realized I had participated in trivializing Sexton's often confessional work, which included titles such as "The Ballad of the Lonely Masturbator" and "In Celebration of My Uterus," because I was brainwashed about poetic language by the literary dictators of the day. They empowered themselves to debase some words and condone others. These were the same professors and critics who praised W. D. Snodgrass's very personal *Heart's Needle*, about the loss of his daughter in a divorce, which received the Pulitzer Prize. As Rich wrote,

> Can art be political and still be timeless? All art is political in terms of who was allowed to make it.

In homage to Adrienne Rich, I invite you to accompany her, among others, in this essay, just as she piloted me around Berkeley in the early 1970s, tie-dyed and wide-eyed, with my knapsack of carbon-copied quotes. But while I read and worshipped Rich, I also wondered why poems by many of the ardently political women were too true—to turn a phrase on its head—to be good.

Two Strands

Our fig tree, cut to the quick six years ago because it would not fruit, has been reborn into a behemoth of a bush, yielding hundreds of figs, close to a thousand, every year. A miracle, in Christian terms, I suppose. A nonbeliever such as myself prefers to believe nature likes to start fresh, rather than prune a bit here and there when things turn grim, hence our decision to risk the life of the tree by leveling it.

Picking the figs fell to Valyntina. Figs contain furanocoumarins, which affect liver and gut enzymes that activate or deactivate drugs, and therefore control the blood levels of many pharmaceuticals in ways that can be life-threatening. Fortunately, the reckless compound is in the milky sap of the leaves and shoots, not in the fruit itself, unlike, for example, in the unwitting grapefruit. But the leaves and root sap of a fig can be very irritating to the skin when one is feeling around in the beating sun for ripe ones, plump and soft.

Around the time Valyntina was risking her tender flesh for fresh fruit, jam, jelly, and pie, I had a wasp problem. Every summer, wasps need water to cool their paper nests, and they found our watering hole. These insects collect and transfer water by swallowing it and regurgitating it into other wasps' mouths, a debased and miscreant version, anthropomorphically speaking, of French kissing. The arthropods were going about their business of staying alive. Unfortunately, they followed me, tormenting me, not intentionally; in fact, they aren't known to pick a fight, but any wasp in a colony will sting multiple times to protect the queen. My pleasure in our sweet fruit shriveled like an oasis in the summer desert when I learned, as nature would have it, that figs are full of baby wasps.

Most fig trees are pollinated by wasps because they are flowering plants in the mulberry family that bloom inside their pods. Since the fig's flower is hidden inside itself, a pollinator, in this case, a fig wasp, needs to crawl into the fig to carry pollen to it. Female wasps need to get inside to lay eggs. The fig emits a perfume that attracts the females, who struggle to get inside through a small opening at the end of the fig. It is such a tight passage that a wasp usually loses its wings and pieces of antennae. It doesn't matter because it will never need them again. It runs around the interior of the fruit visiting many flowers, laying its eggs and spreading pollen. The wasp lays her eggs and dies. Her male offspring, blind and wingless, mate and then burrow a tunnel for the new females to fly out with fertilized eggs and pollen in search of a new fig.

Edible figs wind up with at least one dead female wasp inside. I learned, fortunately, that the ficin enzyme dissolves the insect into proteins, which get absorbed by the plant, so it is seeds being crunched as one chews, not bugs. Anyway, it turns out that not all figs are created the same.

The Kadota fig, our beauty, which dates back 10,000 years to the Jordan Valley, near Jericho, does not need pollination for fruiting. Such parthenocarpy, from *parthenos*, virgin, and *karpos*, fruit, is also true for Black Mission, Brown Turkey, Brunswick, and Celeste figs. These so-called "persistent" or common figs are all female, don't need to fertilize to fruit, and the fruit has no seeds, as with some cucumbers, tomatoes, oranges, grapes, kiwis, bananas, and blackberries. Of these fruits that develop without fertilization, it is the common fig that, according to Jewish legend, was the forbidden fruit on the tree of knowledge, and not the infamous apple.

Although I am not a Christian and don't practice confession, I report that, upon learning that our fig did not need our wasp, we drowned the wasps and poisoned their papery nest. Selfishly, I reclaimed the yard. As a Jew, I have a lot of guilt about it. Where Christians believe they are born sinners, because of the original transgression of Adam and Eve, Jews believe that man [sic] enters the world free of sin, with a pure soul. Only slowly does she determine to exterminate a colony of wasps.

I was living between two strands of Jewish identity: the Jew as radical visionary and activist who understands oppression firsthand, and the Jew as part of America's plan in which the persecuted, called to assimilation, learns that the price is to engage in persecution. Adrienne Rich

Exposed?

Insofar as I am a destroyer of wasps and a conduit of some privilege, I enact power. How best materialize, dispel, or reimagine this in art? The standard I saw represented in anthologies of the twentieth century, bereft of any but a few women, resulted in alternative presses and compilations to repudiate a norm which privileged certain material, tones, and styles over others. Recently, *Sinister Wisdom* celebrated forty-five years of publishing. In 2015, Cherríe Moraga revisited her preface for the fourth edition of *This Bridge Called My Back: Writings by Radical Women of Color*, a 1981 groundbreaking anthology. The best writing in these iconic collections, and many nascent journals and anthologies, serves as correctives to dominating aesthetic sensibilities by deconstructing them with reinvigorated and newly imagined associations and connotations in language.

I believe that when we posit a movement of women, a movement both conscious of our oppression as women and profoundly aware of differences among us, ... we enter a realm more complex than we have moved in before, so that the very questions about literature become new questions.

These "new questions" permitted new freedoms and responsibilities. It is still indeed a "complex realm." But poetry is rooted in human behavior, deeply common. In their rebuke to cynicism, poems are natural, sensual, and as familiar as porch light or bare bulb. At other times, like searing sun, candlelight, or fog. We fall under a spell, as writer or reader, not always aware that each form of illumination comes with inherited assumptions. Who is lucky enough to have a porch? Is it screened-in cedar siding, or rotting planks and loose steps? And where would a speaker be under a bare bulb? Prison? A laboratory? That is, how does poetic usage tend to mask bias, and does usage necessarily differ across identity groups?

Current practices in identity politics discredit some of Rich's 1970s feminism as essentializing, imposing white bourgeois feminism on all women. One person's carefully considered theories on life and art may be inadequate and blind to the next generation's, or next person's, practice. As Audre Lorde posited, "It is not our differences that divide us. It is our inability to recognize, accept, and celebrate those differences." In effect, she asks the old questions: Who gets to say what poetry is, what poetry is for, and what is a "good" poem?

> *Theory—the seeing of patterns, seeing the forest as well as the trees—theory can be a dew that rises from the earth and collects in the raincloud and returns to earth over and over. But if it doesn't smell of the earth, it isn't good for the earth.*

I consider myself an ardent feminist. Yet I have been ambivalent about what Anis Shivani, in "Notes on the Ascendancy of Identity Politics in Literary Writing," describes as literary culture:

> Literary culture, like the academy in which it resides, seems to be moving toward a harder multiculturalism, wherein the claims of identity assume the first order of priority. In the process, literary writers have felt themselves increasingly pressured to take public stands on such vexing issues as affirmative action, undocumented immigration, and various forms of exceptionalism, not to mention increasingly sharp categorizations of sexuality.

He goes on to quote Korean American writer Chang-rae Lee:

> Has there been a form of literary affirmative action for ethnic writers, and, if so, has it ultimately hurt more than helped us? Has there been a backlash to multiculturalism? Have we been ghettoized as writers of color, and has that been the book industry's fault, or our own? Are white

writers, when appropriating other races or cultures, treated differently? Is that kind of appropriation ethical? If we stopped writing about race and made our characters non-race-specific, would it lessen attention to our work? Has the subject of race been a crutch, lending an artificial urgency and weight to our books? Without it, would many of us be exposed as not very good writers?

My own wavering support of identity politics in poems didn't prevent my writing lately about older women's invisibility. Perhaps I tell myself that I describe, rather than polemicize or rhapsodize about my group. I wish the category of "lesbian poetry," as the category of "women's poetry," etc., was not necessary. I know this is naive and dangerous, as voices in support of basic human dignities sometimes need to be heard in unison to be heard at all. I admit that I was hypercritical of what I felt was whining in a lot of late twentieth-century poems absorbed with regret, resentment, and anger. Some "women's liberation poetry" read, for me, as hand-wringing, followed by vagina-opening. I'm no prude, but I preferred my eroticism with a slit up the side rather than up the front. Put less glibly, *less like a sexist man*, I preferred my investigations to play out in a lyrical meditation, not in a narrative demonstration of an ethnically homogenized biography, a discourse that can become shallow and one-dimensional. I think it was Wallace Stevens who said that sentimentality is a failure of feeling.

Sacred Text?

I found in the lyric experience more original diction and more experimental syntax, which serve poetry's relationship with essences and its inclination toward multiplicity and paradox. Trained to foreground the romantic lyric, I soon learned sometimes it is insufficient. The atemporal pretensions of art can be disastrous. Without historical context, without reality, poems can participate in the debasement of some words, and elevation of others, with serious consequences.

> *I understood finally that this heroic will to endure is still not the same as the will to change, the true rebellion.*

When I think of rebellion in the arts, I'm reminded of Louise Glück's comment that the process by which experience is changed—heightened, distilled, rendered—has nothing to do with sincerity. "The truth, on the page, need not have been lived," Glück tells us. "It is, instead, all that can be envisioned." My favorite recent works are by C. D. Wright and Claudia Rankine, whose powers of empathy equal their powers of imagination, whose narratives are lyrical, and whose lyricism is demonstrably documentarian. Their work is as intent on advancing their relationship to words as to their lives and causes. Their sentiments ultimately do not fit a pattern.

Clare Coss's publisher billed her 1996 publication, *The Arc of Love: An Anthology of Lesbian Love Poems*, as "the broadest, most erotic, most sophisticated collection of lesbian love poetry." *Publishers Weekly* described its problem:

> Coss, a psychotherapist, neatly quarters material into sections that follow the letters of the word love (light, order, vexation, and endurance/evolution/ecstasy). Coupled with simplistic introductions to each section, her "arc" resembles a 12-step program in which weaker poems are included because their sentiments fit the pattern.

I allow that I let the anonymous reviewer deter me from reading the anthology, but whoever wrote it invites one of the questions asked by Anis Shivani's essay in *Subtropics*: "If we can classify much of the new canon as testimonial, then is it sacred text, or is it subject to critical analysis?" Has the twenty-first century, exhorted by feminism, the "me-too" movement, and identity politics, made divisions into literary groups inevitable? Are some of these groups above suspicion? Why wade into this miasma? Fiddlesticks.

Hey Diddle Diddle

A fiddlestick was originally a violin bow. Shakespeare used it in a proverb, "The devil rides upon a fiddle-stick," in *Henry IV*, meaning that a commotion has broken out. A little linguistic slippage leads to the broomstick upon which witches, allied with devils, are reputed to "ride." Typical of the anxiety over witchcraft, the fifteenth-century theologian Jordanes de

Bergamo reported: "The vulgar believe, and the witches confess, that on certain days or nights they anoint a staff and ride on it to the appointed place or anoint themselves under the arms and in other hairy places." Indeed, witches must have felt certain they were flying after applying what, in effect, were boiled hallucinogenic plants to their vaginal area with long swab sticks, accounting for the iconic image of sorcerers astride them. A broomstick was probably also used to stir the concoction. But according to anthropologist Robin Skelton, the whole broomstick and witch connection is more likely rooted in the pagan ritual of farmers leaping and dancing astride pitchforks, brooms, and poles to encourage their crops on the night of a full moon.

The witch in one engraving by the Italian artist Parmigianino is not riding a broom, but rather a gigantic phallus. John Marston, Shakespeare's contemporary, likewise extracts sexual innuendo from the stave for Antonio's courting in his satirical play *Antonio and Mellida*: "O love, come on, untruss your points, / my fiddlestick wants rozen." Woman as witch, devil, object, and sexual satisfier. It isn't until the Protestant Reformation, with bans on drinking, dancing, and brothels, that depictions of witches and their brooms in the art of the day relegate them to domestic work. Women, also words, can be debased quickly or slowly over time, on purpose or by neglect.

The illustrious fig, conveyor of mythology, has been much maligned by the quaint, reductive phrase "I don't give a fig," which term, when defaulted to at all, means, "I don't give a shit." Its variant, "I don't give a fig's end," referencing the insignificant nub at the end of the fruit, recalls the corruption of "fiddlesticks" to "fiddlestick's end," at least according to Francis Grose's 1811 *Dictionary of the Vulgar Tongue*; if this producer of dictionaries is to be trusted—given that, as former governor of New South Wales, he established military rule, abolished civil courts, and failed to stamp out the practice of paying wages in alcoholic spirits (a failure admittedly somewhat compelling)—one may bemoan with him that the trifling tip of the bow has come to express "a thing terminating in nothing." No one prevented the debasement of the word!

Rogues of the exclamation "Fiddlesticks!" have devolved from the jargony "bunk," "baloney," and "bull"; the quaint "poppycock," "balderdash," "malarkey," and "drat"; and the disparaging "nonsense"; into popular vulgar corporeals: the disreputable "crap," perverse "horseshit," and terse "nuts." Losing some of its figure but none of its color, the slangy "Oh, fiddlesticks" has morphed decisively into one of English's most abiding interjections, the pointed, grandiloquent, foreshortened "Oh, fuck."

After politicians, charlatans, and versifiers diluted variants of the noun "fiddle," it didn't take long to debase and popularize its verb form, "fiddling," enacting gross sexual behavior, and then, with some overlapping, "diddling," as in Henry Miller's misogynistic *Tropic of Cancer*, rife with stuff like: "He may not have fucked her at all, but she may have let him diddle her." In some cultures, child molesters are called fiddlers, and their heinous sexual abuses "kiddie-fiddling" and "kiddie-diddling." The assonant words sound flippant but are vile and malignant in their degraded versions. As to the Mother Goose rhyme

Hey diddle diddle,
The cat and the fiddle,
The cow jumped over the moon,

according to British literary critic Dr. Oliver Tearle, it probably originated with a game involving a "cat," which was a piece of wood struck with a bat, played to accompanying fiddle music. Apparently a version of the game was enjoyed by medieval monks and nuns. It seems that a cat playing a fiddle was a common image in early medieval illuminated manuscripts. But a less savory literary history is reported for the cat and fiddle from an anonymous, and likely corrupt, internet source. The unrefereed site, itself a degradation of serious archival research, claims that the Mother Goose rhyme first appeared in print in the late sixteenth-century collection, *Focke Ye And Th'orse Thou Rode 'N'Upon and Other Bawdy Recytes*. The researcher opines that "to hold the fiddle" means "to grab the rigid penis like a bow."

So much for the dignity of fiddlesticks and fiddling. As to diddling, once prominent in Gaelic lilting, or singing in dialect, as "tremble" and "shake," it was to be further besmirched in the limerick "There was a young man from Toulouse / Who thought he would diddle a goose . . ." Finally, the same errant website's charlatan claims to have found a 1548 poem by one Lawrence Benjamin, who seems, perhaps generously, to have vanished from literary history. In it, the female heroine emphatically urges women of all classes to diddle, or masturbate, with the line "Laydees auf all strypes, pull up thyne skorts and diddle thyne quim."

Today's fiddlestick makes what's referred to as a melodic sound, another reduction and appropriation, given its origins in African percussive beats and Cajun music, wherein a second person taps out rhythms with sticks, straws, or needles on the fiddle's upper fingerboard. The strings are struck while not tuned to specific pitch, and therefore generate a polyrhythmic sound against the valorizing of simple, sweet, lyrical melodies. The whole debasement of fiddlesticks, involving the debasement of women, musicians, children, and witches, reminds me why it is necessary to maintain an ethical relationship to words.

I'm Gay

Here is an excerpt, a snapshot of narrative, from Kitty Tsui's "A Chinese Banquet," which I empathize with, and have myself experienced, but which I would not want to have written:

. . . she no longer asks when I'm getting married.
one day, wanting desperately to
bridge the boundaries that separate us,
wanting desperately to touch her,

tell her: mother, i'm gay,
mother i'm gay and so happy with her.
but she will not listen,
she shakes her head.

Some poets have to deal with the informational level of reality, getting the story out, plain and simple. It is hard for me to reconcile with a feeling that a poem is about more than one thing at a time. Sometimes about more than one time at a time, and more than one kind of figurative language. For me, Tsui's piece lacks nuance and intrigue, it is predictable. It is also sad and empowering, but it is not as radical in its language as it is in its politics. Compare it with the opening of danez smith's family poem "saw a video of a gang of bees swarming a hornet that killed their bee-homie so I called to say I love you":

honey bitch
you kin me
so good I would
kill on sight
if you asked
gun knife or bite
a man down
to bloodnectar

One can't miss the compound "bloodnectar." The invention startles me viscerally, like a paper cut. The diction is reminiscent of Paul Celan's jagged compounds, several of which explode in the 1959 volume *Speech-grille*. Among those Pierre Joris rendered into English: "crowswarmed wheatwave," "worldblind," and "hourwood." Celan's diction implores us that imagination is an antidote, not only a companion, to reality. Many self-serving poems from the merely personal, righteously actual world sacrifice this complexity, but sharing this feeling occasionally embarrasses me and hurts others. It's not that I don't understand that we need transcriptions of personal experience, protected by political alliances. The dignified grassroots work of women, for example, has finally led to them being singled out for achievement. The work is hardly finished.

After years of an imperative to dismantle, among infamous publishing structures, a two-tier system of "female poets" and "poets," the hierarchical nomenclature still exists. I welcome with impatience the unmasking of deeply entrenched biases in publishing, the academy, and the awards industry. While those benchmarks have been almost mooted in the arts in general, the literary arts in particular, and poetry most especially, as the humanities are stripped of respect and funds, it has never been more important to reevaluate systemic bias in them. The combined efforts of many marginalized artists, including trans and Black activists, have worked to legitimize and value every poetry by elevating their own sectarian themes. I tell myself I do my part by representing the claims of the older woman I have become.

But is it a violation of others' sensibilities to argue for multiplicity, to stray from my "lane," as I have, in my way, proceeded to: "Americanize" the haiku; universalize the suffering of traumas I've only witnessed or read about; disregard most criticism while sometimes engaging in it; feel scholarship to be full of jargon while "performing" lectures (this book), notably without credential; mock surrealism while exploiting it; etc.

Does it mean that I am cautious around "birds of a feather flocking together"? It is said that this phrase was popularized by a Dr. William Turner, celebrated, also imprisoned and banished, for promoting the reformation of the Church. His 1545 parable, *The Rescuing of Romish Fox*, announced, "Byrdes of on kynde and color flok and flye allwayes together." In a barely disguised polemic praising his fellow (sic) reformers, he employed the pejorative term "papists" to label his opponents, thus hierarchizing one flock over another. Banding groups together, which currently includes the "branding" or commodifying of groups, has both positive and negative valence. Older sources of the parable include Plato's *Republic* and also Ecclesiastes: "Birds resort to their like." Generalizing, hierarchizing, and grandstanding, not to mention the nefarious dehumanizing that is blind loyalty, have diluted the best intentions of group empowerment for centuries.

Faint with Love

The first fruit mentioned in the Bible is the fig, in the company of a nightingale and turtledove in the sublime love poem "The Song of Songs":

Behold, the autumn has passed,
*   the rain has gone, blossoms are seen in the land,*
the time of the turtledove and nightingale has come,
*   the fig has formed its first fruit;*
the vines in blossom give forth fragrance.

The poem celebrates sexuality, also devotion and marriage. Not quite ready to marry when asked, a woman regrets sending her male suitor away and is determined to find him:

My beloved thrust his hand through the latch-opening;
*   my heart began to pound for him.*
I arose to open for my beloved,
*   and my hands dripped with myrrh,*

my fingers with flowing myrrh,
*   on the handles of the bolt.*
I opened for my beloved,
*   but my beloved had left; he was gone.*
*   My heart sank at his departure.*
I looked for him but did not find him.
*   I called him but he did not answer.*
. . .
Daughters of Jerusalem, I charge you—
*   if you find my beloved,*
what will you tell him?
*   Tell him I am faint with love.*

The poem is as much a love song to nature as to a beloved. When the male returns, the rains stop, the trees blossom, and the nightingale sings in the shrubs. What could go wrong?

Your lips drop sweetness as the honeycomb, my bride;
*   milk and honey are under your tongue.*
The fragrance of your garments
*   is like the fragrance of Lebanon.*
You are a garden locked up, my sister, my bride;
*   you are a spring enclosed, a sealed fountain.*

While the maiden declares herself "opened for my beloved," her lover describes her upon his return as a "spring enclosed," "garden locked," and "fountain sealed," establishing the relationship between chastity and femininity. She's beautiful, she's perfect, and her desires are quickly corralled and controlled. Metaphor is a linguistic site particularly vulnerable to manipulation. As a student of feminism, I learned that lyric poetry, a marvel of airy images, could mask profound disturbances in the representation of the female.

Just a Kiss

The nightingale is nearly always characterized as female, melancholic, and a night singer, often with its breast against a thorn. These are myths that serve to romanticize and fetishize the female, who, in fact, is mute. Poets have used the bird as a muse for centuries, projecting their own ache onto it. The failure of a trope is familiar to those who have been misrepresented and objectified in art and life.

I have never maintained that heterosexual feminists are walking about in a state of "brainwashed" false consciousness.

The English Romantic poets have a particularly dark conception of the nightingale. Milton is typical, personifying the songbird as female and lonely. In *Paradise Lost*, "the wakeful Bird / Sings darkling, and in shadiest Covert hid," while "Il Penseroso" enforces the pervasive bummer mood, "In her sweetest saddest plight . . . Most musical, most melancholy!" Coleridge does his best to unravel the connection of nightingale with melancholy, and indeed with poetic tradition and myth:

And hark! the Nightingale begins its song,
"Most musical, most melancholy" Bird!
A melancholy Bird? O idle thought!
In nature there is nothing melancholy.

Young Keats talks of suicide to his nightingale. The poem opens,

My heart aches, and a drowsy numbness pains
My sense, as though of hemlock I had drunk,
Or emptied some dull opiate to the drains
One minute past, and Lethe-wards had sunk:

Drinking hemlock, as Socrates was forced to do, sounds attractive to Keats, especially after he nursed his brother through the last stages of tuberculosis the year before. When Keats hears the nightingale, he longs to follow it and to "cease upon the midnight with no pain," motivated ultimately neither by drugs nor alcohol, but by an imagination which, in the end, fails him. As the bird flies off, he can no longer recall whether its music was "a vision, or a waking dream." Pouring forth its soul, the nightingale is Keats's ecstatic companion and symbol all too briefly.

In many poetic guises, the bird is a dark mystery and balm, swelling the hopes and calming the nerves of poets, naturalists, children, and soldiers with its sweet crescendo. But the mythic Philomena of Ovid's *Metamorphosis* has another destiny. She is not like the female bird, naturally silent; her tongue has been cut out so she won't reveal that she was raped by her sister's husband. Paisley Rekdal's 2019 book, *Nightingale*, takes up the theme:

> Just a kiss, he says, dropping his tackle box, and I know I should run. He grabs my head, and I am already clawing at his head, terrified but also terrified of hurting him. Hurting him will make it worse for me. He hisses in my ear as I slap his hands, and now he's got his arms around me. I rear back, unbalancing myself, so that when I do the one thing I've been taught, which is to bring my right knee up hard into his groin, the blow is weak.

Rekdal's sharp details, the tackle box, the clawing, the frantic doubling of "head," "hurting," and "terrified," are an attempt to inscribe what happened. She frankly examines being brought from speech into silence by the rape, unable to get her original body back:

> Language is the first site of loss and our first defense against it. Which is why after Philomela's brother-in-law, Tereus, rapes her, he cuts out her tongue and tosses it, the bloody stump hissing at the girl's feet.

Philomena's revenge begins when she weaves a tapestry to reveal her rape. She begs to be transformed into a bird to escape Tereus's rage at being outed. Because of the violence associated with the bird, its song is often construed as a lament. Rekdal at first is similarly voiceless and seemingly powerless in her contemporary poem.

> *The word power is highly charged for women. It has been long associated for us with the use of force, with rape, with the stockpiling of weapons, with the ruthless accrual of wealth and the hoarding of resources, with the power that is only in its own interests.*

Rekdal implores the reader: "I want you to give me what no one can give me." Finally she realizes, in "Nightingale: A Gloss," "Only language, which orders time and gives experience shape and meaning, might control how violence is experienced. It gives back agency." Rekdal's language is variously intellectual, lyrical, and narrational. In employing the nightingale, her poem becomes a study on voice more than an indictment of evil.

That's Why It's a Sin

Among classic North American songbirds, we have the finch, wren, warbler, and thrush. Homing in on the American Southwest, where I live, the songbirds are swallow, purple martin, goldfinch, cactus wren, towhee, warbler, and thrasher. The thrasher makes itself more conspicuous than the rest, dashing about in the open, sporting a loud *whit-wheet*, which some say sounds like a whistler hailing a taxi. The towhee has a sharp, pinging note, according to the *Audubon Field Guide*, while *All about Birds* claims that the cactus wren sounds like a rusty old car cranking. I hear it as a creaky screen door. The finch, who loves sugar water and sunflower seeds, has a chirpy warble.

For those like me who have never heard a nightingale in nature, birders say that the Mexican whippoorwill's sweet, insistent call is close. The trill of a mockingbird is even nearer the flute-like nightingale's, according to *Audubon*, but the bird will imitate car alarms and cats and get annoying. Nevertheless, there are ardent supporters of the mockingbird, among them Harper Lee's fictional Finch family, not coincidently Lee's mother's family name:

> Atticus said to Jem, "I'd rather you shot at tin cans in the back yard, but I know you'll go after birds. Shoot all the blue jays you want, if you can hit 'em, but remember it's a sin to kill a mockingbird." That was the only time I ever hear Atticus say it was a sin to do something, and I asked Miss Maudie about it. "You're father's right," she said. "Mockingbirds don't do one thing but make music for us to enjoy. They don't eat up people's gardens, don't nest in corncribs, they don't do one thing but sing their hearts out for us. That's why it's a sin to kill a mockingbird."

Among enthusiasts and metaphorizers, it is the nightingale's song, bright as a silver flute's upper registers, which has reached iconic status. The hype gives little real agency to the actual female, bound up as it is in myth. Not only is it the male who sings, the song is sung by day as well as night. Apparently, the male's repertoire increases dramatically with age; so much for generalizations about youth's virility.

The nightingale's flute, a variety of whistles, trills, stops, and gurgles, is becoming as rare as the eerie pitch of an ancient flute made from the ulna bone of a red-crowned crane. Such a wing bone was unearthed in China, at Jiahu, the site of a Neolithic settlement and, carved, is said to have beautiful glissando up and down. Were such cranes found dead, dissected, and crafted, or were they captured and killed to make music? Now, the red-crowned crane is severely endangered and under protection, so the flute cannot be reproduced. The nightingale population is likewise devastated, unnatural human behavior having destroyed its territory. According to *The Guardian*, the population has plummeted by 93 percent in England. With its connection to nature severed, the figure's final codification will be emptiness or martyrdom. Once ubiquitous and still idolized, the mellifluous creature itself is somewhat dun.

More exactly, the common nightingale is cocoa or milk-chocolate colored, a hue derived from orange, red, green, and blue, formally known as dark-grayish tangelo. The color of many tree branches, the bird is hard to locate in the wild or in a backyard, and never in North America, but has flourished not only in poems but in songs, fairy tales, operas, and novels, revealing who gets to sing, and of what use, or punishment, silence is.

In Igor Stravinsky's *Nightingale* opera, the bird accepts an invitation to entertain an Emperor, but says that its sweetest song remains in the forest. The Emperor adores its sound but, when gifted with a mechanical bird that also sings, casts off the original because it is less handsome. It is only when the Emperor wakes to find death sitting on his chest that the nightingale returns to restore him. However, despite offers and orders, it rejects an invitation to stay forever, for the bird wants the freedom to sing anytime, anywhere.

Mourning the Wound

The nightingale was also a particularly popular poetic subject and authorial emblem in the eighteenth century for "lady poets," as they were often disparagingly referred to, among them Sarah Nixon, Catherine Talbot, and Mary Robinson, all of whom wrote elegiac, reticent, and self-effacing plaints. However, Elizabeth Singer Rowe's use of the pastoral space, especially in "A Pastoral Elegy," is transgressive, where Daphne, a water nymph, is lamented not by a grieving shepherd, but by another nymph, Philomela. This was groundbreaking, brave, shocking diction. The mythic bird shows unusually frank lesbian agency in a poem that now sounds quaint. Language can be a corrective force, but it is also subject to manipulation, cliché, and hyperbole:

She's gone, she's gone, my dear Companion's gone,
And left me in this desert World alone;
Unfore't, her Beauteous Soul has took its flight,
Serene, and Glittering to Eternal Light.
More blind than Love, or Chance, relentless Death,
Why didst thou stop my charming Daphne's Breath?

Out of context, that is, out of date, the purposeful adjectives, "serene," "beauteous," "glittering," and "charming," lose their lightning. The speaker's desperate affections are aggrandized further because her lover is pursued and harassed by the god Apollo, to the point that she begs to be transformed into a tree, the laurel, a particularly popular woody plant in which to posit a nightingale. Paisley Rekdal has re-contextualized the fetishizing of the bird:

> The nightingale hovers between trauma and memory, its song meant to bring one into concert with the other, to integrate event into narrative, to bring pain out of the body and into language.

Rekdal is thinking of the consequences of lyricizing the reality of pain, trauma, and harassment:

> In life, time's passage allows us to see change, but a poem's chronology forces us to see repetition: lyric time is not progressive but fragmentary and recursive. Traumatic time works like lyric time: the now of terror repeatedly breaking back through the crust of one's consciousness. Mourning the wound thus becomes an obsessive love for the lost.

A long-standing belief in the elegance and intensity of the lyric poem has kept me from fully embracing the documentary in poetry, even as I understand the necessity for stories. Why? Self-sabotage? Elitism? Ignorance? I should remember that it was Sappho who announced, "If you are squeamish, don't prod the beach rubble." However, just as we have to commit to a vigilance over what lyric subjectivity takes for granted or unknowingly reinforces, we are accountable to the realm of the senses as we record our histories.

The continuing spiritual power of an image lives in the interplay between what it reminds us of and our own continuing actions in the present.

Disclosed by the Stars and Silence

Many current anthologies featuring lesbian poems exist, too numerous to document here, except by cherry-picking a few to indicate their depth and breadth. Two twenty-first-century collections: *The World in Us: Lesbian and Gay Poetry of the Next Wave*, from St. Martin's Press in 2000, features poems by recognized voices, Robyn Selman, Olga Broumas, and Eileen Myles among them, and emerging artists such as Letta Neely and Melanie Hope. And here is an anthology just printed as I write, which I look forward to reading: *The World That Belongs to Us: An Anthology of Queer Poetry from South Asia.*

One of the most impressive lesbian poems appears alongside work by Cheryl Clarke, Judy Grahn, Adrienne Rich, May Swenson, Tatiana de la Tierra, Honor Moore, Joy Harjo, Dorothy Allison, Kitty Tsui, and Marilyn Hacker in a 1988 collection edited by Carl Morse and Joan Larkin, *Gay and Lesbian Poetry in Our Time: An Anthology*, also featuring James Baldwin, W. H. Auden, and Frank O'Hara. This is from June Jordan's explosive "Poem about My Rights," including the right to move about safely and freely:

alone because I can't do what I want to do with my own
body and
who in the hell set things up
like this
and in France they say if the guy penetrates
but does not ejaculate then he did not rape me

and if after stabbing him if after screams if
after begging the bastard and if even after smashing
a hammer to his head if even after that if he
and his buddies fuck me after that
then I consented and there was
no rape because finally you understand finally
they fucked me over because I was wrong I was
wrong again to be me being me where I was/wrong
to be who I am

A rush of lyrical repetitions rachets up Jordan's narrative maelstrom. Her grievance is not expressed as idea, but as event, which mounts to a brazen crescendo in a series of run-on, unpunctuated sentences. The poem continues on an ever-expanding scale to name international atrocities, then ends with a massive threat:

... I can tell you that from now on my resistance
my simple and daily and nightly self-determination
may very well cost you your life

Jordan's fury is impossible to cast off as a fleeting vernacular riff; her song is heroic, her grievances, against sexism and racism, systemic. Insofar as they are still a problem, they must be solved by all of us.

"As a woman I have no country. As a woman I want no country. As a woman my country is the whole world." These words, written by Virginia Woolf in her feminist and anti-fascist book Three Guineas, *we dare not take out of context to justify a false transcendence and irresponsibility toward the cultures and geopolitical regions in which we are rooted.*

The Curved Breast

The first known agricultural crop, figs made their way into artist's imaginations before wheat, barley, and legumes in poems, drawings, and paintings. But religion and convention have often had a hand in showcasing a fig's leaf for unsavory purposes.

In Masaccio's *The Expulsion from the Garden of Eden*, while Eve covers her nudity with her hands, it's interesting that Adam has elected instead to cover his eyes, perhaps so as not to see her, leaving his genitals exposed. Eve appears ashamed, her keening mouth and squinty eyes eternally stricken. Adam is bowed and equally miserable. Some Jewish texts describe them as glorious, but obviously not the young Florentine frescoist, who died soon after he finished the work, only twenty-six years old. Over two centuries later, church leaders, in a sign of their seventeenth-century times, ordered fig leaves painted on the couple.

Michelangelo's *Last Judgment*, a fresco of three hundred figures covering the altar wall of the Sistine Chapel, including a voluptuous St. Catherine among other naked forms, met a similar fate earlier when Pope Pius IV ordered loincloths and fig leaf coverings during the Church's "Fig Leaf Campaign" of 1563. Likewise, Peter Paul Rubens covers Eve, although not a seated Adam, with a fig leaf in *The Fall of Man*. Titian covers both young torsos in full-summer overgrown leaves in his version, and in yet another *Fall of Man*, Michelangelo—who, remember, painted Adam and Eve eating a fig in the Garden, not an apple—parks Eve demurely at Adam's feet, torqued to one side and, forgoing the fig leaf, crosses her legs to cover her genitalia. Eve eyes the serpent keenly as she accepts his forbidden offer. To read into her gaze may involve more than Michelangelo intended. Be that as it may, the artist depicts Adam gloriously naked. I can't help but think that painter and subject are both reveling in getting away with it.

The valorization of manliness and masculinity.

It was a different Michelangelo nude, *David*, carved from a single block of white marble and installed in the Piazza della Signoria in Florence, that offended the authorities. The naked torso was girdled almost immediately with a garland (a *ghirlanda*) of copper fig leaves around the giant's waist, a *cache-sexe* ("hide-genitals" in French), a small garment like the Western G-string or Japanese *fundoshi*. David wore his modesty wreath for over a hundred years.

While some literal damage can be repaired, Michelangelo's *Last Judgment* was destroyed forever a year after the artist's death when his student, Daniele da Volterra, scraped the nudity off some of the vilified ("all lasciviousness") in a waterfall of figures during the application of fresh plaster on which to paint fig leaves and veils. Michelangelo's visionary act survives only in a copy, a tempera painting on wood.

Countless other artistic creations and their social responses variously controlled the discourse around the nude figure with the presence or absence of the large, broad, flat leaf, whose sandpapery, serrated edges and small stiff hairs scratch their subjects and rankle our imaginations.

The nineteenth century loved its men dressed and its women naked in paintings, but we wait well into the twentieth century for a sexy, rare reversal of the Garden of Eden's guilty figures, Tamara de Lempicka's twentieth-century highly stylized Art Deco version. It is said that the artist, inspired by a female who took a break from modeling nude to eat an apple, completed the iconic tableau by inviting a policeman on patrol to pose as Adam. Though nude, Adam's back is to us, covering one of Eve's breasts with his bicep while embracing her, who is otherwise, for all intents and purposes, finally full-frontal naked and undaunted at Inception.

As for those two lost souls of Masaccio, they had their "bandages" safely removed by art restorers in 1988. Barefoot, broken, unequal, but once again naked, they walk despairingly out of the ontological woods onto yellow desert sands.

Starred with Premonitions

I imagine that it might be the excellent Kadota fig tree toward which their walk of shame leads. The scene looks to be near Jericho, with the Jordan River to the east and Jerusalem to the west. The southern Levant region is mostly desert and dry steppe. The Taoist mystic Gao Pu, a poet and collector of strange tales, wrote about the value of camels in the difficult environment:

The camel . . . manifests its merit in dangerous places;
it has secret understanding of springs and sources;
subtle indeed is its knowledge.

Poetry, too, has secret understandings and subtle knowledge and is especially protective in dangerous places. It serves as a guide to our most complete selves. When I heard that the image of "a camel's nose" alludes to the old Arabic saying "Don't allow a camel to put his nose under the edge of your tent, for soon you will have a camel in your tent," I heard an allusion to poetry. Despite the potentially sinister implications of intrusion, in an open, safe society the activity is innocent, and in art making entirely necessary. Creation is all about "breaking-in"; that is, groundbreaking, disruptive acts are the lifeblood of originality. Disruption can be a form of "right conduct" in the same way the I-Ching speaks of change and transformation as underlying all existence. To disrupt is to break free from convention, conformity, expectations, and judgment.

I reject, too, the proverb's other negative interpretation, in which a small, seemingly innocuous act opens the door for larger, undesirable actions. I suggest that "the undesirable" might simply be "the new." Of necessity, context is everything; I'm not suggesting that brute force should determine who directs language. But in the deepest recesses of the artist's soul, no matter the social setting, one must be combustible and energetic, one must be free, as Paul Celan announces in "Discus": "Starred w premonitions / throw yourself out of yourself."

Airy Nothings

Practicing poetry can be perilous. The independence of the artist is always in danger of being at something's or someone's expense. I prefer the healthy term "interdependence," where having an awareness about otherness frees us to be our best creative selves. When I'm silenced by guilt, powerlessness, or ignorance, or am overwhelmed by inherited symbols and meanings and lose my instinctive voice, lose, that is, my desire, I think of Zbigniew Herbert's extraordinary poem "To Ryszard Krynicki—A Letter," where "we came too easily to believe beauty does not save." The whole phrase goes:

we came too easily to believe beauty does not save
that it leads wantons from dream to dream to death
none of us was able to wake the dryad of a poplar

It is heartbreaking to be unable to wake the dryad, or spirit, of a tree, typically female in legends. Heartbreaking not to hear her pure recitation. Has this personal lyric urge inadvertently or purposefully contributed to the patriarchal framing of archetypal imagery? In response, have narratives become overwhelmingly didactic? If lyricism is infamous for crystallizing the symbology of the patriarchy, and narrative indulgent in affirming the politics of aggrieved cultures, poets will seek further breakthroughs in consciousness and composition to elevate the discourse. Can language be free of damaging stereotype? Presentation is ripe with possibility and rife with consequences.

Because I've never heard a nightingale's aria, and likely never will, I imagine it sounds no more beautiful than the little tweeter, a goldfinch, chirp-warbling outside our kitchen window in the fig tree, not in sad or melancholic tones, nor does it attach to any mythology. What it's doing is strategizing about how to feast on our bounty. I take its song, and its hunger, to heart. For the North American who has no access to a nightingale's habitats, nor cares to carry its burden of meanings, it is a gesture of respect to substitute the local flyer for the abstract icon. For the poet, it is a linguistic necessity to declaw patronizing or oppressive figures and also to return declawed, misappropriated icons to their original wildness, as when Judy Grahn came to reclaim Marilyn Monroe's body. Here is poet and critic Anis Shivani again:

> This is, perhaps . . . where academic collegiality is incompatible with imaginative writing, which most would agree is nonconformist, solitary, often opposed to community or citizenship or even responsibility, and in general driven not by any optimistic political agenda but by darkness and light in equal measure.

Poetic language is a song worth liberating, rather than controlling and caging. But the choice may be beside the point as metaphor converges with reality. We are silencing ourselves by destroying our home. As of now, heat waves in the desert are putting its native songbirds at grave risk of extinction. A newspaper report on Christmas Day, 2020, verifies that flycatchers, warblers, and swallows, including the mellifluous violet-green swallow and the boisterous purple martin, literally fell out of the sky in a mass die-off in the southwestern United States in September and October. Starvation and dehydration are killing the singers and their song. Heat that we exacerbate is aggressing onto mountaintops, trees, and shaded washes, the last refuges.

I report this with outrage and fear. In contrast to blameless birds falling from the sky, I'm reminded of the self-inflicted fate of Icarus, who, in his hubris during an attempt to escape Crete on his father's wax invention, flies too high, melts his wings, and falls from the sky into the sea. Our own abuse of nature enacts the Edenic metaphoric fall from grace. Humans are responsible for reductions and distortions of the natural world and its language. To avoid arrogance or hesitation, and instead be fully awake now, is to resist human fear and moral failure. Under new terms of engagement, as creators, we have got to imagine a possible future for song in nature and in poetry, both of which enact death and life in each start and stop of musical phrase. Inside that music, a practice of ritual and commentary survives.

Poetry's lasting form, the ode, puts us in reach of things and people through one of the most beautiful emotions, praise. It has been criticized as mere rapture, and, according to the Russian writer Alexander Pushkin, lacking tranquility. Ironically, Pushkin was hero to one of the world's experts at animating objects, Pablo Neruda, whose odes, beginning with the first of three books, *Odas elementales*, in 1954, celebrate onions, horses, salt, socks, soap, dictionaries, and rain, among so much else, including my favorite, "Cordillera de los Andes," a song of the Andean Mountains, site of ancient America, "defending the snow of its star." Neruda's homages are to the earthy nature of language itself. Shakespeare explores this succinctly in *A Midsummer Night's Dream*:

And as imagination bodies forth
The forms of things unknown, the poet's pen
Turns them to shapes and gives to airy nothings
A local habitation and a name.

Foliated Scrolls and Little Bells

Optimally, the language of poetry protects the link of the common to the unfamiliar. I think of the figure of the camel crossing that awesome desert, inspired by its literal crossing of intractable terrain from the bustling market and trade center, Xi'an, the start of the ancient Silk Road in north central China, to the Mediterranean, one generation after another for over fifteen centuries. I admire the expressiveness of the camel and its stamina in transporting valuable goods.

Its devotional history is impressive. Prior to service in the silk trade, camels hauled frankincense and myrrh along old incense trade routes from around the time of Homer's *Odyssey*. And camel bones excavated at Timna, in the Sorek Valley near Jericho, reveal that they hauled copper from mines in the early years of the Iron Age, around the 10th century BC. In a quirk of fate, these indefatigable workers have been commemorated cast in metal. New York's Metropolitan Museum, for example, houses a stunning three-inch bronze Bactrian, or Mongolian, camel with its atypical double humps, as opposed to the dromedary's single bulge. It is a compact block of head, big-lipped snout and highly stylized neck, stout torso, front and rear legs cast as one, and two legendary upside-down "pails" in which to store fat, and not, as lore has it, water, for nourishment over the long journey. Water is carried in their oval-shaped blood cells, which are elastic to accommodate more liquid. The revelation emboldens us to question received knowledge of the camel; of life, also art.

Bronze, an alloy of copper and tin, but also arsenic, phosphorus, aluminum, manganese, and silicon, produces a substance much harder than copper alone. And bronze alloys have the unusual and desirable property of expanding slightly just before they set in a mold, thus filling in the finest details. At the Louvre, two gilt-bronze, that is, gold-finished, bronze camels sit facing each other, andirons made for the Turkish boudoir of Marie Antoinette. They appear to be smiling, or at the very least, unladen and relaxed, enjoying an afterlife as decorative art:

> Their chasing renders a camelhair effect, along with the details of their saddlery. The bases they rest on are decorated with beading that echoes that found on the friezes of the wainscoting. The fronts are made up of foliated scrolls and little bells beribboned with gilt.

An indulgence? A pleasure? Art is often enjoyable, sometimes functional, dangerous, or empowering, and always expressive. As art objects, bronze camels ablaze with artifice signify stamina and sacrifice, at rest in a queen's bedroom or defiant on the corner of 13th Street in Vancouver, where they commemorate grunt work in the gold trade. If the camel presents as ugly or alien in art history, culture, and mythology, it is another misjudgment by those in power, another failure to accept difference and rarity. In fact, camels are the most endangered large mammals, that is, next to us, according to the World Health Organization. The camel serves as a beast of burden for pilgrims and worldly goods, but also as a metaphor, a conveyor of our selves across the vast unknown of our lives. Bronze camels are also found among ancient *mingqi*, small sculptures buried to serve the dead as guardians in the afterlife. They are like poems in conveying sacred material. As bronze is to raw copper, poetry is an amalgam, a magical, combinatory agent, much stronger than speech because more refined, more flexible, and lasting.

Javelina Stink.
What I Dare Not Say about Poetry

Javelinas are not rodents. They are pig-like hoofed mammals, also known as peccaries. They may be distant relatives of the wild pig, but they stink in their own special way. While pigs are malodorous because of hydrogen sulfide, ammonia, and methane released in digestion, javelinas reek to survive predators and separation. That is, these coarse-haired mammals release a strong musk to rub the scent on rocks and tree stumps to mark their territory and to identify each other because they don't see well. They especially rub their babies, known as reds, and will charge you if they feel their young are in danger. In moonlight, in profile, their short legs and long torso appear weirdly two-dimensional. Like pigs, fourth in intelligence behind monkeys, dolphins, and whales, javelinas are smart. While Texans treat them as vermin and do not eat them, Arizonans love them with garlic, achiote paste, chipotles in adobo, and ground cumin.

I hear javelinas are delicious because they eat mesquite beans, prickly pear, agave, roots, tubers, and other green vegetation, also pale green, or Kadota, figs, about which I can personally attest. I watch every summer as the herd stink-bombs my courtyard tree, bumping their snouts into low branches and giant leaves and upturning rocks for fallen, buried fruit. They hunt with their great sense of smell, which may lead you to wonder if their own emanation offends them. It seems not, judging by their slow nosing around in close herds. It seems paradoxical, not unlike, if you will allow me a far-fetched simile, a poem, which doesn't know whether it stinks or not. Permit me awhile to nose around poetry, with the sincere hope that I will not offend.

1. Not Every Comparison Is a Simile

Speaking of similes, let's remember that not every comparison is a simile. "She looks like you" compares two related subjects, but "she smells like barbecued javelina" is a simile. Take, for a much better example, the wonderful Robert Hass poem, "Heroic Simile," whose first stanza travels miles and centuries:

When the swordsman fell in Kurosawa's Seven Samurai
in the gray rain,
in Cinemascope and the Tokugawa dynasty,
he fell straight as a pine, he fell
as Ajax fell in Homer
in chanted dactyls and the tree was so huge
the woodsman returned for two days
to that lucky place before he was done with the sawing
and on the third day he brought his uncle.

The poem spirals on a couple of similes, each abandoned, and ends where it began, outside a movie theater playing a film by the Japanese master, Kurosawa. Here is the surprise ending:

A man and a woman walk from the movies
to the house in the silence of separate fidelities.
There are limits to the imagination.

Come to think of it, the first, or the first two, of these lines could have stood as an ending, but only one is formidable, maybe objectionable, and clearly arguable, and that is the last, which tells us, in the case of the couple, whom we have only just met as the poem closes, empathy only goes so far and things are dire. Or are they? Maybe couples are often loyal elsewhere, and possibly survive, or thrive, that way. Or the poet isn't commenting on conjugal life at all, but rather on the poet's, and possibly the filmmaker's, dilemma that it's not possible to solve every creative problem. In any case, if we leave aside the couple, much may be considered about the sentence, "There are limits to the imagination." Are there limits? What are they? When are there limitations, and has Hass shown, for this poem, that the imagination is limited? The poet announces at some point, "I have imagined no pack animal / or primitive wagon" to help two characters haul wood in the poem. At another point, the poet-speaker admits, "There is nothing I can do." By abbreviating various plotlines, Hass enacts his limitations.

The poet has accounted for the ending, but also prepared us to think and feel beyond it. While Robert Hass admits he can pursue a scene only so far, the poem has taken us deep into an associative slippage to inquire about creativity itself. Many poets tend toward analogies, the point of an analogy being not merely to show, but to explain. In that way, a poem puts an end to our interest in it, whereas great poetry is limitless. Hass walks the couple home "in the silence of their separate fidelities," with us equally rapt in our own opinions and limitations.

2. All Poetry Is Love Poetry,

at first impulse, by which I mean, the act of writing is an act of creation that is essentially positive in nature. The requirement for writing a poem is an openness to music and words, and the requirement for reading a poem is an interest in connection. The intimacy shared by participant and author might be characterized as curious and attracting. Whether a poem pursues an argument, tells a story, creates imagery, collects chance elements, or enacts itself in prose, it works with ancient tools, including lists, repetitions, sound relations, spacing, lineation, and associations. These tools are designed to energize. The language arts are a social experience unto themselves, emanating from the friction of creation, one letter of the alphabet propulsing another, word by word, phrase by phrase. Not surprisingly, any assumption about individual letters is both confirmed and belied by their company. I hate to say it, but many poets forget the extent of, and limitations of, the English alphabet.

First of all, lest we forget, very few letters exist in English. Five vowels, a handful of weird consonants that are striking for how rarely and queerly they are used—the j, q, and z chief among these—and varying combinations of the rest of the more versatile consonants compose the whole tool kit. The charm is in their sounds, and with it the possibility for communal figures that poets continually adapt, enshrined as long ago as the first cave scrawls. A group of majestic horses and boisterous rhinos from the

Ice Age, 30,000 years ago, stunned contemporary explorers of the Chauvet caves in southern France, but they also found semicircles, lines, and zigzags that, far from being doodles, are in fact highly symbolic, forming a written "code" that was probably familiar to the prehistoric tribes around France and possibly beyond.

The whole operation of combining these (by now, long-codified) semicircles, lines, and zigzags into words is unstable and volatile. New word combinations are always emerging, even as some formerly archetypal signs drop "off the cliff" into cliché (like that one) and are avoided "like the plague," a cliché if I ever heard one, and inappropriate at that, given the pandemic years in which we are living. At any rate, the event of a poem is highly kinetic. You might say that one's relationship to language is incomplete, so poet and reader enter a shared place that calls for patience, trust, and intimacy—love's triad.

I admit that, to me, writing poetry is a form of love relationship because I often personify the letters of the alphabet, experiencing them as companionable, cherished friends with different personalities and skills. I love having them over and the quiet when they leave. I hate when I don't pay enough attention to them in the moment, and it bothers me when other poets lazily choose words with little sense of their open, clenched, or explosive effects. Letters of the alphabet have an inherently lively quality when meshed together and vocalized. They hum in the throat, growl in the jowl, pinch the face, relax the jaw, squinch the eyes, tickle the nose, cluck, whimper, oooh and aaah, etc. In short, they create sensation in our bodies, which in turn resonates like strings strummed or hollows blown. We respond to a physical act when we enter the sounds, stops, glides, bumps, and echoes of a poem and commit to reading for their sense and sensibility.

For the maker, this requires a respect for the alphabet in which one is working, its capabilities and shortcomings. We must imagine how it sounds to think and feel as we do. If one is a reader of poetry, what begins as a desire to listen to something may become an opportunity to hear oneself.

3. A Lot of Poets Are Tone-Deaf

Saying a poet has a "tin ear" is insensitive and unfortunate because a "tin ear," made of soft, slivery metal, refers to the arcane "ear trumpet" for the audially challenged that now has been reduced to a gag gift. "Tin ear" loosed from its referent smacks of disrespect. Is "tone-deaf" another insulting "ableist" term? It is the case that a spell is lost or absent in a line of verse if a poet isn't paying attention to sound. Lazy, clunky sentences in a popular contemporary form, the prose poem, haven't helped. A poem is marked by a time signature, loose or firm, that performs an event in a space, while its effects are experienced as a suspension of time and a floating in space. "Let's get lost," as crooner Chet Baker suggested, as we listen to part of a lovely John Clare poem, "I Hid My Love":

I hid my love in field and town
Till e'en the breeze would knock me down;
The bees seemed singing ballads o'er,
The fly's bass turned a lion's roar;
And even silence found a tongue,
To haunt me all the summer long;
The riddle nature could not prove
Was nothing else but secret love.

Of course, you're hearing the formal verse of another age. Perhaps it seems quaint to you, with its end rhymes and steady iambs. But the gait of the poem, gently dependable, has caught the spirit of a gentle nature, who had a secret, kept it, and only later discovered it was love. It's at once tender and delightful.

Clare's poem's regular pace and deeply felt conviction about the power of love ("even silence found a tongue") employ some of the more rounded sounds of our alphabet, especially the "o." A naturalist and solitary, John Clare suffered fears and delusions, which led him to exile himself in an asylum at High Beech, a village inside Epping Forest, for four years. Eventually homesick, he walked the eighty miles back to his wife and seven children, eating grass to stay alive. It wasn't to be his last confinement. I have to ask, John Clare, may we hold you in our hearts if we cannot hold you in our arms? Here, art and life come perilously and miraculously close together.

While Clare's mind grew frailer, his ideas about poetry strengthened. Observing the natural world and its social institutions, he compared grammar to slavery, often resisting standard spelling, capitalization, and punctuation that were replaced by editors. He wrote of regional edibles and medicinals, geography and meteorology, and, as a farmer's son, could predict the weather from the lovely, although poisonous, scarlet pimpernel, as in his *Shepherd's Calendar*, whose forecast from the month of May includes over three hundred lines of weeders, flowers, bats, grass, brooks, wheat, and dozens of birds:

And scarlet-starry points of flowers
Pimpernel, dreading nights and showers,
Oft calld "the Shepherds Weather glass"
That sleeps till suns have dyd the grass,
Then wakes and spreads its creeping bloom
Till clouds or threatening shadows come—
Then close it shuts to sleep again;
Which weeders see and talk of rain.

Though he is the quintessential poet who esteemed the earth, in other ways, unfortunately, his connection to reality kept slipping. He imagined a second wife and took credit for Shakespeare's plays. Eventually, he suffered schizophrenic episodes and spent his last twenty-three years at St Andrew's Asylum, in Northampton, where, some say, he wrote his best poems. Among the most poignant is the self-titled "To John Clare," whose soothing iambic opening no one, sadly, dare risk now:

Well, honest John, how fare you now at home?

At home in the world in his own mad way, he was intent on preserving local dialect, employing terms like "thacking" for roof covering, or, as in this stanza, "clock-o'-clay" for beetle, winking at its reference to time:

In the cowslip pips I lie,
Hidden from the buzzing fly,
While green grass beneath me lies,
Pearled with dew like fishes' eyes,
Here I lie, a clock-o'-clay,
Waiting for the time o' day.

In another context, Clare's image of a "cowslip bud" is erotic: "Cowslip bud so early peeping . . . ," which continues with Clare's idiosyncratic punctuation,

Ah for joys thoult there be meeting
In a station so divine
Id 'most wish thats vain repeating
Cowslip bud thy life were mine

The terms "nature" or "natural" poet, once quaint, now fashionable again, hardly do justice to John Clare's role in unabashedly exploring love and the erotic, as if his closeness to nature would preclude human intimacy. He has proven intimate with any speech, preserving language and inventing words, including the onomatopoetic gem, "children pace the crumping snow," for the sound of frosted snow, broken by play, in one of his Christmas poems. Pointedly, his nightingale in "To the Nightingale" is no courier from a golden version of pastoral, in some magical invisibility, but grounded and earthy. It sings not from a beauteous glade but "Where mugwort grows like mignonette, / And molehills swarm with ling." The grunts and hard angles of his poems especially remind us of our humanity.

A fluid passageway channeling our experiences exists between writer and reader, plied by twenty-six couriers. In such a way, the spirit of John Clare is delivered to us. Poets who put flat prose into lines of verse, or assume a prose poem is an excuse for caterwauling, miss the whistle of departure of their ferry and the ensuing undulation of waves. They miss *moving us*, emotion and motion being the same.

4. Time Is Very Different Here

is a sharp line from Linda Gregg's poem "A Letter." Sharp, that is, it marks a demarcation in the poem. The poem barely pauses, but everything contends with this sentence. The rest is more personal. The poem opens, "I'm not feeling strong yet, / but I'm taking good care of myself." A voice emerges and sounds trustworthy. Is that what we look for in a poem? Not necessarily. Here, the ending comes up quickly:

Time is very different here. It is very good
to be away from public ambition.
I sweep and wash, cook and shop.
Sometimes I go into town in the evening
and have pastry with custard. Sometimes I sit
at a table by the harbor and drink half a beer.

The end is beguiling. Why tells us the pastry has custard? It seems a trifle. (Perhaps it literally was a trifle, originally an alcohol-soaked sponge cake with custard? Gregg is not one to waste words.) This custard arrives courtesy of the prepositional word, "with," potentially adding an unnecessary abundance to a spare poem, a poem that has been, impressively, about sloughing off worldly concerns. But the detail slows the poem's ending, as does the repeated "sometimes." "Half a beer," too, implies an excruciatingly slow time. Ordinary one-syllable words and declarative sentences fill the structure, like a whitewashed room with little furniture, uncurtained windows, and a simple picture or two on the walls.

Yet the poem includes several mysteries, beginning with an unknown addressee. Is the letter written, we are made to wonder, to someone who knows the speaker well or little? Has the intended recipient figured in the plot, that is, is the recipient in some way responsible for the speaker's sojourn elsewhere? Perhaps we readers take a little time, while the character sweeps and washes, to think about that. I feel renewed by the basic actions of the speaker, but it is still not the reason the poem moves me.

In fact, to discuss time, while enacting the way it moves when we lead a quiet life, turns this into a big poem. It is accomplished with diction and syntax. I fear that many poets aren't thinking enough about time in poetry, which includes the time of the line, the time in the setting of the poem, and time in the mind in the poem. One can imagine the speaker nursing that glass of beer, distracted, ultimately only getting half-through. In addition, the excess of dessert, as she takes her time, and ours, in its pleasure, suggests what is missing, regarding pleasure, from an obviously sensual life, at a remove from an unmentioned other time and place. While the speaker feels the difference between one place and another, the reader regards absence and presence, until death itself is a consideration. Whatever the speaker is missing and recovering from, "taking good care of herself," haunts the calmness of the scene, as time's eventual cessation haunts our most intense experiences—"la petite mort," for instance, originally the phrase for a fainting fit or nervous spasm, more popularly refers to the "little death" of orgasm.

It seems that the more Linda Gregg's speaker itemizes her present, the more suggestive the rest of her world becomes. Gregg's slowdown of action is poignant. "Sometimes I go into town in the evening"—the casualness leaves out so much that has occasioned this healing. Time gets a real workout in poetry, expressed in a space lattice. Elements surface that have been glossed over or barely alluded to. So much in Linda Gregg's letter about the present suggests the past and the future. Space imitates time in poetry. It is what makes every deliberate poem potentially tragic. Unfortunately, most personal poems don't want to risk this ultimate self-effacement.

A poem asks, are there points of time, or intervals? Some events in a poem stop the flow with a jolt. Other language events flow skittishly or rapidly. Centuries may be alluded to quickly, or a moment might gigantically leap territory, as in the Italian poet Eugenio Montale's "News from Mount Amiata," a Tuscan volcano, written around the time he finished the "Motets," twenty enigmatic love poems. This has a similar desperateness:

I write to you from here, from this distant
table, from the honeycomb cell
of a sphere hurtling through space—
and the hooded cages, the fireplace
where chestnuts explode

Montale vaults us into outer space and back to his room where a fire burns, apparently inside him as well. It appears that the present is central, but in the time of reading it, we really experience a state suggestive of many realms. Time is very different in a poem because there is so much of it: the lost time that we live in the art event; the time evoked in it; the time spent afterwards under its spell; and especially, the irretrievable time from a life we might have lived, had we not been altered by the poem. The resultant "new time" gifted me by virtue of changes wrought by the poet is the most exciting. A fourth wall comes down in the theater of our lives, where we've been reading poetry, and we find ourselves inquisitive, unsteady, and overwhelmed by the majesty of a new perception. Or else it's not a poem, as Charles Bukowski remarked, it's typing.

5. Movements Suck

By the time a literary movement gets named, defined, and argued, it has forfeited its value for artists. To find one's own voice, or style, or bearing—essentially the same things—is a noble endeavor, and while it may involve understanding classifications intellectually, writing is not prescriptive. The whole point of living as a creator is to be original. Not that I mean we find our way, only to repeat it endlessly; that would be to get better and better at the same thing. I suggest, inferring from writers I admire like Virginia Woolf, Marguerite Duras, and Gertrude Stein, that it's better to develop from project to project than to improve the old one. I think it was John Berryman who spoke of this in *The Life of the Poet* and enacted it in the leap he made in the 1960s—not to be confused, forgive me, with his suicidal leap—from *Homage to Mistress Bradstreet* to *77 Dream Songs*. *Bradstreet* combines a provincial, seventeenth-century simplicity along with "jagged intellectual probing," as Robert Lowell calls it. *The Dream Songs*, on the other hand, are sloppy, nervous, and weirdly obsessed with a minstrel language long past acceptable, but they afforded Berryman, as alter ego "Henry," to be as anguished and deranged as his syntax:

But never did Henry, as he thought he did,
end anyone and hacks her body up
and hide the pieces, where they may be found.
He knows; he went over everyone, & nobody's missing.
Often he reckons, in the dawn, them up.
Nobody's ever missing.

David Wojahn, while a huge admirer of Berryman, describes Berryman's later poems as "a wacko mixture of Elizabethan contrivance, heaped-on literary allusion and bald self-disclosure." It isn't easy to keep changing and growing as an artist, but at the very least, the effort is, as Lowell said, "a drive against the barriers of the commonplace."

What we make, in the end, is one body of work, noticeably ours. A life's work is an intrigue as it emerges, periodically codified into a movement by a critical apparatus often exaggerating or misaligning commonalities among the makers. Not for us to say or care. One can't walk away from lovers, family, or friends cruelly and indiscriminately, but, as Jon Anderson once wrote, "The secret of poetry is cruelty," which I take to mean that each work is unabashedly a new act, which involves no looking back. Everything learned from one's former projects is brought forward anyway, so why fret? One can hardly live one's life abandoning and destroying human relationships with a sharp cut, but as artists we must be severe. Someone will decide later how your new poem was inextricably tied to some pattern, some "ism." We can let the space of creation be absent of opinions. What of this majestic, empty state?

Where a bricklayer or road paver is driven by finances to complete a job "on time," artists have to find a way to get off the clock to write. Paradoxically, this may mean finding "extra time" in the day, rising in the middle of the night or before dawn. As the clock disappears, we enter a free zone of composition and contemplation. It is a wonder. We become unguided and unguarded. Like all such states, say, of prayer, meditation, or lovemaking, you prepare all you want, but then intuition, curiosity, and mystery take over. Of course, many tasks can be approached "artistically," with fine attention to detail. Many bricklayers or window washers, for instance, approach their jobs with integrity about method and finished product. Expertise is a rare and beautiful accomplishment. (Occasionally one files one's taxes "creatively," although that provocation is for another conversation.) But for artists, with our signature deliberately all over the thing, our allegiance is to the process itself, not the accomplishment, before it is shapely and "like" someone else's. Poets obsessed with their product, their finished poem or manuscript, as to where it will be published and how received, misjudge the mission. Shakespeare said it—"Ripeness is all." The making is to be savored.

Jorie Graham has spoken about how mysterious a process it is that a poem changes by simply breaking its lines differently. She goes through innumerable drafts of reformation until her line of poetry is the signature of her line of thought. This resolution is yet one more thing that is unearthed from a deep, inexplicable territory. Even an awkward experiment has more chance for a breakthrough in consciousness than a proscriptive act obeying yesterday's latest evaluations. Beyond former and current movements, your next poem is the least conspicuous, most rapturous place. Paul Celan wrote about "Standing in the Shadow":

To stand in the Shadow
Of the Wound's-Mark in the Air.
For no-one and nothing to Stand.

6. Irony Is for Wimps

We poets have all resorted to it. Camouflaged as humor and wit, irony works as a pause, a surprise, a conundrum, even a comeuppance. Irony gets readers to backtrack deftly over terrain, as its rhetorical gesture creates slippage and doubt. The reader becomes a "player" in the poem; that is, the reader must choose what the poet "really" means, and take the same side, rather than look the fool.

But more exactly, what is an ironic moment in a poem? Irony is the contrast between the surface meaning and the underlying meaning. Sometimes irony lapses into sarcasm, which is aggressive. More often, when the poem says one thing and means another, deliberately understating or misleading, the poet intends to set it right by the end, where the obverse may be revealed as true. But much that ensues sews confusion.

Chet Baker's famous tune "I Get Along Without You Very Well (of course I do)," starts to make use of not-meaning-what-he-says, but the lyrics quickly become less sarcastic the more the song obsesses on exceptions to the refrain, including "except when soft rains fall," or "maybe except when I hear your name," and so on. Baker's dropping from the sublime to the ridiculous, that is, from the truth to its variants, contradictions, exceptions, etc., isn't at the audience's expense; the situation is unmasked immediately. The irony is so gentle that there's no ruse at all. The genuineness of the heartache of his song has attracted Billie Holiday, Diana Krall, and Nina Simone to record it.

Contrarily, when the ruse is the rule, the audience as interlocutor becomes variously accepting and suspicious as the writer advances gambits. Advantage is gained as the lyric proceeds. It seems rather competitive. Typically, the participant, the listener, is brought round, maybe exhausted by the experience.

Robert Frost's "The Road Not Taken" is a classic example, an iconic American poem that annoys the hell out of me, as it is very clever and screams with irony, beginning with the title. Frost might mean, for one thing, the road not taken *by others*. Consider that Frost intended the poem as a critique of a romantic friend, the wonderful poet Edward Thomas, who Frost thought always regretted decisions made. But Thomas's poems reflect physical and metaphorical landscapes, where satisfaction lay frustratingly up ahead or on the road "not taken." It is worth a moment to listen to lines from "Liberty":

And yet I still am half in love with pain,
With what is imperfect, with both tears and mirth,
With things that have an end, with life and earth,
And this moon that leaves me dark within the door.

Perhaps this recognition of "otherness" Frost ought to have valued. So, one reading of the more famous poem is that it's mean-spirited. But that's not what annoys me. The poem is, in fact, about delay, given how each road is a bit more like, than unlike, the other anyway.

We readers go back and forth considering them with our traveler, who might want to come back and try the other if he could, but then he'd not be the same for having taken the first one first, yet another irony. The poem ends on the further irony that the road taken "has made all the difference," but we don't know if that difference was better or worse. Underneath the "noble" choice that the poem documents lies the parodic poem, a takedown of somebody who can't make a decision. An even more generous reading of the poem is that the speaker knows he'll be judged later for whichever choice, and we should have some compassion about that. But ultimately, the poem seems to me to be busy tripping up its audience. The poem is saved by Frost's great control over the music, featuring a nearly three-stanza-long opening sentence. Then, after an exclamation—"Oh, I kept the first for another day!"—the poem continues to its ironic conclusion:

Two roads diverged in a wood, and I—
I took the one less traveled by,
And that has made all the difference.

Frost seems a real smarty-pants here, using tools that are not to be confused with dramatic irony employed in plays and novels, where the audience has more, rather than less, information than one of the characters. Take Othello, who doesn't know that his Desdemona has been faithful. Also different is situational irony, as in Coleridge's "Water, water, everywhere, / Nor any drop to drink." Big ocean, undrinkable. That's true, and it mitigates the irony.

You won't catch Federico García Lorca or Paul Celan dropping into the ironic mode to move their poems along, confusing and undermining various propositions, arriving smugly. They are too unrelentingly intent on tragedy. No feigned ignorance surrounds Lorca's poem "Farewell," for example, which, by adding only a final exclamation point to its cry, begins and ends with an entreaty: "If I die, / leave the balcony open!"

7. History, Science, Philosophy & Religion Need Us More than We Need Them

I've been in a quandary about bold, rhetorical commentary in poems, and the risks involved in declamations, ever since I read the legendary advice of Rilke's written over a century ago that famously ends "Archaic Torso of Apollo." It is tempting, as a poet, to want to make commanding declarations. Rilke's poem features the god of music, poetry, prophecy, and healing, albeit without a head. Nevertheless, the torso mysteriously sees us. It seems the essence of the poem is the stone itself. At first, the reader is mentioned only briefly, in relation to the torso, which is "suffused with brilliance from inside. . . . Otherwise / the curved breast could not dazzle you so." Again, about the stone: were the stone not lit from within,

. . . this stone would seem defaced
beneath the translucent cascade of the shoulders
and would not glisten like a wild beast's fur:

would not, from all the borders of itself,
burst like a star:

What bursts, if taken out of context, sounds like advice from your trusted friend: "change your life." But it is a surprise because "you" were never at issue, until you suddenly center the poem. This reorientation is the beginning of modernism. The reader is addressed almost as an interloper. Maybe because Rilke was exploring sculpture then, working as Rodin's secretary, he is suddenly able to swivel the poem to "you," as one might go around back of the chiseled stone to see all of it.

With the abrupt shift to address you directly, the poem invites a new perspective, like a scientific theorem, a spiritual insight, or "bio" art, the latter an approach which introduces the biological sciences into the plastic arts. But one needn't adopt Rilke's diaphanous and prophetic voice nor study the sciences to risk a grand statement. Neither need one make such a statement. It is often a decision requiring not courage, but reserve, which Rilke exhibits by focusing on the marble, not philosophy.

Frank O'Hara isn't known for his reserve. He says outrageous things about art, for instance, in "Having a Coke with You": "the portrait show seems to have no faces in it at all, just paint / you suddenly wonder why in the world anyone ever did them." His nonchalant delivery is famously charming and intelligent. His poems act casually, conversationally, with bare punctuation. They sound jocular. Yet a lot is at stake emotionally, and some things need to get said, and this is precisely when he speaks reservedly, as in his last major poem "Biotherm":

. . . being available

it is something our friends don't understand

if you loosen your tie

my heart will leap out

. . .

why are you melancholy

if I make you angry you are no longer doubtful

if I make you happy you are no longer doubtful

what's wrong with doubt

Whereas some intellectuals need an affected lyricism to be understood, the poet doesn't need to wax philosophical or graft scientific jargon magisterially to be intelligent. O'Hara simply drops a last inquisitive phrase into the poem.

Adrienne Rich, more intense than nonchalant, is well known to incline toward commentary. Her critics did not find her ideas the stuff of poetry. She wasn't encouraged to think at all by her first "supporter," Auden, who wrote a shameful defense of her first book: "The poems a reader will encounter in [Rich's first] book are neatly and modestly dressed, speak quietly but do not mumble, respect their elders but are not cowed by them, and do not tell fibs." Many remain unmoved by her social, gendered, historical poems risking what philosophers find naturally appealing, ideas, as in her 1962 poem, "Translations":

You show me the poems of some woman
my age, or younger
translated from your language

. . .

I begin to see that woman
doing things: stirring rice
ironing a skirt
typing a manuscript till dawn

trying to make a call
from a phonebooth

The phone rings unanswered
in a man's bedroom
she hears him telling someone else
Never mind. She'll get tired.
hears him telling her story to her sister

who becomes her enemy
and will in her own way
light her own way to sorrow

ignorant of the fact this way of grief

is shared, unnecessary

and political

I remember the liberating effect of an encounter in another of her poems when I was a young woman attracted to women while living with a man. In "Dialogue," two women talk frankly about their sex lives. The intimacy cuts through chatter. The space between the two friends is palpably inviolate. The poem concludes:

I get up, go to make tea, come back
we look at each other
then she says (and this is what I live through
over and over)—she says: I do not know
if sex is an illusion

I do not know
who I was when I did those things
or who I said I was
or whether I willed to feel
what I had read about
or who in fact was there with me
or whether I knew, even then
that there was doubt about these things

The poem breathlessly outpaces its statements with repetitions—the "I," for both women, almost a dozen times—and a run of interrogatives (who, what, where, when) and conjunctions (or, whether). The dialogue is conversational and flat, but the poem glides on clauses of anaphoric energy. The effect is revelatory rather than expository. And what is revealed but deliberately not stated? Is the friend admitting that, as a part of heteronormative pressures, she has faked orgasms? Rich re-signified what was appropriate material for poems. Any poet choosing the declarative for bravado, who isn't writing beyond the farthest extent of her knowledge into the unknown, isn't living fully.

One could go all the way back to Dante to see the poetic landscape festooned with ideas about what life is, what a good life is. Although he did consign Aristotle, "the master of those who know," to hell, Dante has plenty of historical, political, religious, and poetic ideas about revelation. He articulates an allegorical journey by a series of encounters, and as the great poem progresses, the advice and commentaries are swift and sure: "Do not be afraid; our fate / Cannot be taken from us; it is a gift." Dante's speaker, even as he suffers confusion in his spiritual epic, *The Divine Comedy*, accumulates surety. The masterpiece is an orchestra of lyrical music embedded in a richness of metaphor. Ultimately, the lessons of philosophical progress are simple, even in hell, from where he says, "The more a thing is perfect, the more it feels pleasure and pain." While a philosopher or scientist has to be an exceptional sentence-maker to theorize lucidly, it is the poet's natural, inner music that leads to ideas. Still, it takes tact and modesty to make declarations, if one must.

We know that for William Carlos Williams, "so much depends upon" creation, and much depends upon our saying that it does, and how to say. In thinking about imagination, Williams, an imagist, produces a less studied elegance than another mid-twentieth-century poet, the symbolist Wallace Stevens, but both exist in a largely pagan world where rhetorical activity, often declarative commentary, is a metaphysical necessity. They advance arguments as they advance pictorials, with musical support.

Their influence extends into the deep reaches of contemporary poetry. Even a list poem shorn of declarative sentences can achieve natural rhetorical energy, as in this excerpt of danez smith's poem "alternate names for black boys," which upends clichés:

1. *smoke above the burning bush*
2. *archnemesis of summer night*
3. *first son of soil*
4. *coal awaiting spark & wind*
5. *guilty until proven dead*
6. *oil heavy starlight*
7. *monster until proven ghost*
8. *gone*
9. *phoenix who forgets to un-ash*

10. *going, going, gone*
11. *gods of shovels & black veils*
12. *what once passed for kindling*

Poets often view the world as they experience it. danez is astute in checking their moralizing, philosophizing and pontificating, but says a lot with slippage such as "guilty until proven dead" and references to first sons and burning bushes. danez doesn't need to flaunt a knowledge of history or to ransack philosophy.

Stevens wrote about how ideas begin in the world in a 1940 letter:

> We are physical beings in a physical world; the weather is one of the things that we enjoy, one of the unphilosophical realities. The state of the weather soon becomes a state of mind. There are many "immediate" things in the world that we enjoy; a perfectly realized poem ought to be one of these things. . . . people ought to like poetry the way a child likes snow.

Maybe the highest form of poetry remains lyrical because "unphilosophical realities" dominate. If, as Wittgenstein supposed, we represent reality through language, that is, if language is reality, how wonderful that poets are born to describe, not analyze. It is Albert Einstein who has this to say about creation:

> The constructions of [the physicist's] imagination appear so necessary and so natural that he is apt to treat them not as the creations of his thoughts but as given realities.

I don't know much about mathematical purity, but Einstein's general theory of relativity feels to have been nurtured by a poetic sensibility. That time is an illusion, that it is relative, are poeticisms of the highest order, although, truth be told, Einstein was a terrible poet. Yet it is Einstein who said that the only reason for time is so that everything doesn't happen at once. His lyrical, paradoxical ideas have made the universe sensorially and magically accessible.

While poetry may absorb some scientific diction, it does seem difficult, without figurative language, to understand, for example, how massive objects cause disturbances in time and space, which we experience as gravity. But there is a simple correlative in one of Rilke's love poems to God:

> How surely gravity's law,
> Strong as an ocean current,
> Takes hold of the smallest thing
> And pulls it toward the heart of the world.

Poetry can also imagine Einstein's cosmic strings stretched across the expanding universe, which bend time and space so vigorously that time travel would be possible. Is not the frisson of traveling to another time an ancient poetic experience?

8. Narrative Poems Are Kinda Sappy

By the way, do you know the difference between a subject and a theme? If the subject is war, the theme might be that war is a curse. A theme carries the weight of a point of view. The theme has moral heft. Put similarly, Vivian Gornick speaks of every work of literature as having both a situation and a story: "The situation is the context or circumstance, sometimes the plot; the story is the emotional experience that preoccupies the writer: the insight, the wisdom, the thing one has come to say."

The chronology of a narrative poem is not what usually interests me. Why? Love and death, two common themes, naturally would seem to demand the elaboration of the beginning and middle to justify its end. But that may take up valuable time in a poem. Goodness knows that we can never feel the sentimental angst or pleasure as keenly as our earnest poet or speaker, no matter how it is contextualized by order. However much we are made to shiver as the action crests and the end approaches, we go on with our lives, like Frank Stanford's cat. The unfolding is uncannily like someone's dream repeated to you, which, despite its surrealism, has a strict chronology which little matters. First this happened, then this, then that, but so what if I ate my lamp before or after napping on Mars? Do you really want the end? Oh, I woke up. A dream, or a poem, is not a detective novel. Of course, most narratives don't want to sound like dreams. But even when being accurate with time and place is of the essence, say, in Louise Glück's "Presque Isle," the poem exudes timeless-ness, concluding lyrically:

That room must still exist, on the fourth floor,
with a small balcony overlooking the ocean.
A square white room, the top sheet pulled back over the edge of the bed.
It hasn't dissolved back into nothing, into reality.
Through the open window, sea air, smelling of iodine.

Early morning: a man calling a small boy back from the water.
That small boy—he would be twenty now.

Around your face, rushes of damp hair, streaked with auburn.
Muslin, flicker of silver. Heavy jar filled with white peonies.

Less imaginative poetic memories would have led, lockstep, to cathar-sis. I prefer poems that jostle with time: "That small boy—he would be twenty now" is ostensibly an aside, but it gives the poem its relativity. Glück mediates the timeline with vivid details, as the devil lies in them. I prefer these flashes of seemingly minor effects that outmaneuver the sen-timental situation of the poem, as when Auden omits not only the story of his visit to a museum in Brussels, in "Musée des Beaux Artes," but also the drama of Icarus's fall from the sky in Breughel's painting on exhibit. Rather, ". . . everything turns away / Quite leisurely from the disaster":

In Breughel's Icarus, for instance: how everything turns away
Quite leisurely from the disaster; the ploughman may
Have heard the splash, the forsaken cry,
But for him it was not an important failure . . .

Consider, too, the marvelous poetic imagination of *Don Quixote*, Cer-vantes's extravagantly rich picaresque novel, which, despite its thousand peculiarities, has little interest in hierarchizing events while "advancing" a plot. Cervantes confers on the illustrious knight a series of loosely con-nected, equally demanding adventures, each of which finds the Don in yet another humiliation that reason would say is rightfully earned.

Quixote, for better or worse, changes very little throughout. Let me just admit, now, that I'm as taken as the next aficionado of literature when a romantic hero, more or less empowered, overcomes, conquers, and sets right. That story line fills like a passenger balloon mounting to a great height, and we stand below on land, rapt and agape. My mouth hangs like the other mouths hang. My eyes moisten histrionically. But contemporary life is rather more episodic than romantic, whose heightened crescendo often turns into so much hot air let out of the aforementioned balloon. On earth, with Quixote, we mount our skinny steeds, trot around the enormous, colorful, collapsing nylon envelope, and continue on, as the shaken passengers spill out the wicker basket and stagger away from an always too-brief escape, disappointed and, forgive the pun, deflated.

So it is that I prefer the antihero, whose heart remains equally noble through success or failure, until time finally intercedes and, undramatically, he dies in his own bed in the end. Quixote's dignified demeanor during multifarious trials ennobles the tragicomedy. We readers fall for him, not out of pity, but out of wonder. The wonder is Cervantes's story, his style. Having all the time in the world, or so it seems, Cervantes has little at stake in ratcheting the intensity. It is like the action unrolling on a Chinese scroll. Each episode has the Zen quality of being "a moment," and is one reason that Quixote himself is a poetic marvel of a man. Hurtling on to the next adventure, his storyteller affords the actor no occasion to rank the be-alls and the end-alls. It's all sharp, even for things distant. Do you, or do you not, see the wild giants in the moment our knight sees them?

"What giants?" asked Sancho Panza.
"The ones you can see over there," answered his master, "with the huge arms, some
of which are very nearly two leagues long."
"Now look, your grace," said Sancho, "what you see over there aren't giants, but
windmills, and what seems to be arms are just their sails, that go around in the
wind and turn the millstone."
"Obviously," replied Don Quixote, "you don't know much about adventures."

For poem narratives, the most challenging distance can be "over there," maybe sixty or a hundred feet away, where things often blur or fade. If Cervantes's text is preposterous and rangy, always in a hurry and never out of time for hundreds of pages, nevertheless it sees everything clearly, if not for what it is, than what it could be. Cervantes has perfected the aesthetic and actual distance, parodying a chivalric tradition, but not its practitioner. It is difficult to achieve Cervantes's loopy music in poetry, that is, both spiraling and maddening; it is difficult to get lost in events but also move through them. The poem may get saggy and pathetic, decorative and sugary. As an anecdote to the reader guessing what's coming, poetry recommends stillness, a pause to contemplate a ladybug on a burl on a redwood deep in the forest, deep in the night. To the poem's point, the story is best told with much omitted.

The ancient Chinese poet Li Po offers tantalizing narratives that remain models of abbreviation with highly metaphorized figures, as in Ezra Pound's free translation of "The Jewel Stairs' Grievance," wherein a woman apparently has been stood up by her lover:

The jewelled steps are already quite white with dew,
It is so late that the dew soaks my gauze stockings,
And I let down the crystal curtain
And watch the moon through the clear autumn.

"Jewel stairs, therefore a palace." "Gauze stockings, therefore a court lady"—Pound's appended notes on the implied narrative. The full appendix is longer than the poem itself! But on our own, we understand she has waited beyond hope. "It is so late" poignantly and delicately expresses her loss, barely alluding to a beloved, a betrayal, a devastation.

What of the epic poem, which has the space to mount a complex story? Perhaps Homer can help us here:

I am a man who's had his share of sorrows.
It's wrong for me, in someone else's house,
to sit here moaning and groaning, sobbing so—
it makes things worse, this grieving on and on.

This scene is near the end of twenty years of Odysseus's cunning and marauding. Penelope soon discovers that the beggar not ready to reveal his past is her long-absent husband. The story will resolve itself in the bliss of their marriage bed, built from the trunk of an olive tree around which the house has been constructed, an image that is more riveting, to me, than the slaughter, which follows, of the suitors and housemaids who betrayed his family. After the goddess Athena joins the battle, the killing ends swiftly. Odysseus spares only a minstrel and a herald. A priest begs unsuccessfully for mercy. All matter of fact. Epic poetry has plenty of hours, feasts, intrigues, and travel, but it does love its close-up of a bed rooted in an olive tree.

Too much filler feels like a lot of nothing in a contemporary narrative, like the minute-by-minute of *Sleep*, Andy Warhol's 1964 avant-garde film, five hours and twenty minutes of looped footage of John Giorno, his lover then, snoring in bed. I would have preferred a sleep broken by an orgy or a lover's quarrel, so I left the theater when I got "the plot," which, strangely but unsatisfyingly, was a long moment of stopped time. Its lyric became narrational! The endless empty lines of breath punctuated unpredictably only by snores nearly put me to sleep.

Another film, Chantal Akerman's *Jeanne Dielman, 23 Commerce Quay, 1080 Brussels*, reminds me of a related problem with chronicles. In hers, we observe a single mother's regimented schedule of cooking, cleaning, and parenting over three days. As part of establishing this rhythm, Akerman has us watch water boil in the exact time of it, and likewise with similar ordinary tasks, scouring, shoe polishing, etc. The tasks, while not, in fact, the same, have the same soporific effect on us, as do too many adjectives festooning stanzas. The quantifying in the film, like qualifying in a poem, is glutinous. When the woman breaks from routine, which includes sleeping with strangers for money, she murders someone. It is, as the distinguished film critic Roger Ebert claims, a great formalist gambit. But the artifice of sterility and sameness that is Akerman's feminist and structuralist critique doesn't explain the self-defeating ending. Perhaps it regards revenge and poetic justice. Yet her film is a cautionary tale to poets about the nature of narrative and its reliance on righteous closure. Certainly, Akerman was brilliant in creating a hypnotic context for content. Ebert puts it beautifully: "The film treats female bodies as vessels that cannot hold all of the radiant female mind and its innumerable intricacies."

Akerman's and Warhol's excruciating visual enactments of ennui in real time use silence, or rather, speechlessness—for there's plenty of snoring and boiling—as soporifics in the grinding of time. In a poem, a reader may not outlast them. I suggest that a saga participate in compact moments. And a short poem dare to feel expansive. These conditions set their respective poems in the direction of frailty, not will. The enactment of ur-reality in the musical vehicle of a poem is, among mirages, a most grand illusion.

If Homer said, as is rumored, that everything ends up in a book, we understand that he needed to repeat certain subordinate clauses formulaically as little choruses, mnemonic devices, because the poem existed within a totally oral tradition, and its singer needed to reset before going on with the song. "When the rosy hand of dawn appeared," "when rose-fingered dawn appeared," "when early dawn revealed her rose-red hands," etc., ad nauseum, had a purpose. Many contemporary poems take too much time, a reader's time, with prosaic directional pointers and prepositional phrases operating like semaphore flags: Under the table, Last night, In the sun, On top of the refrigerator, Whenever he drinks, When she got fired, etc. These prepare us for, but may keep us from, action, emotion, and music.

"Jojo's," Christopher Davis's poem about his brother's murder, veers quickly out of its main narrative, spare with modifying phrases, the closer it gets to tragedy. First, we get the "journalism" of the piece:

The night my brother was stabbed,
But not quite stabbed to death,
I was drinking wine in a coffeeshop

"Stabbed" represents the first, but not the last, doubling and lyricizing of diction. The coffeeshop's name, "Jojo's" (itself a doubling), will appear twice, as will other details, as a way of stopping time. The full poem itself is two stanzas. The first has declarative, flat lines telegraphing a few facts with indicators: "in a coffeeshop" and "On May 1st, / he died in the hospital." The poet's grief is held tightly in check. But where does the story go from there? Into a minor chord after a stanza break:

I've forgotten if I had a good time that night
with my friends. I probably did.
We were all in a band together.

A month later, I
left that town to go to college.
The rest of them moved too, I think.
No, on a trip home at Christmas
I saw Nancy at Jojo's. (They had
found my phone number in his pocket.)
I don't know what
was said, if we did talk.

"I think," "probably," "no," "I don't know," "if"—these seemingly off-handed qualifiers, while deferring rather than distracting, turn our attention from the traumatic story line, whose one last reference the poet has hidden in parenthesis. It would be too much to make much more of the horror. The difficult work of resistance, the moment, for example, spent revising when the speaker last saw his friend, instead of reliving the crime, speaks volumes. Memory blurs as the poem lowers its volume. It seems that a grim or rapturous story in a poem can be told without expounding, without expanding the problem. You might even say that a story in a poem exists for its evanescence. As Robert Hass said in a *Paris Review* interview, "The will can make prose, but it can't make poetry."

9. I Don't Read Contemporary Poems

OK, I admit, I skim them. Much current poetry builds to a foregone conclusion, often foretold. Too many facts get in the way of the whole truth, by which I mean, in the way of the undecipherable, the mysterious. After a few facts, many a worthy poem rushes into some actual—albeit exclusionary—violent act, exploiting the details. On the other hand, poets who resist action resist history, and suffer for that choice by writing a poem that is an exercise. Lacking a subject, these poems are busy with wordplay or tone. It is a difficult time to be a poet. But it usually is.

Since a poem is naturally synchronous, absorbed with more than one thing, it's my view that a hint of the intent of the poem appear early. By "intent" I mean the soul of the poem, its humanity, or, let's face it, the soul of the poet, which, in certain poems, may be the poet's voice. I could have said the mind of the poet, or the style, which speak to the integrity of the emotion brought to bear on the poem, if not necessarily in the poem. So, let's call it the bearing of the poem, which answers to, What is at stake?

What is at stake ought to be of this time and place, and beyond. "Beyond," the word itself sounds haunting and dated, like Poe's "Nevermore." I rather mean that poets write from a present that feels very much prophetic and futuristic, as if we have a secret, an intuition, about life. And we do! We have the words for a possible world, as Don Quixote had his visions. It cannot hobble itself with nerves. I get excluded by poets who identify themselves as victims of their past. I am sorry for their losses, but the more a self consumes a poem, the more limited the poem's arc of intention. I've done it myself. It is the least attractive form of confession. It is a lonely grief, and a lonely argument with anxiety.

Many contemporary poets don't know where to start. Or end for that matter. They could consider Louise Glück's apparent ability to begin at the end, with an intelligent rejoinder to a poem not yet visible. Most readers aren't going to wait for a sensibility, or a music, where none is promised.

Resilient poems start connotative activity immediately, even at a blockbuster title. I'm reminded of César Vallejo's "Piedra Negra Sobre una Piedra Blanca," which Robert Bly translates as "Black Stone Lying on a White Stone," an associative, elemental jewel of a title, with symbolic implications of night and day; political implications for race; aesthetic implications for sculpture, nature, materiality, anthropomorphism; etc. Huge!

Can you believe Vallejo's first line is "I will die in Paris on a rainy day"?! A complete surprise. A tour de force of a surprise, instead of a description of voluptuous white and black monuments, or pocket-size pebbles, or discs stacked in a field, warehouse, or synagogue. Would that be as enviable a poem? Vallejo dares to travel very far, from the connotative to the indicative, from title to first line. The title actually denotes as well as symbolizes, adding another synchronic event, if you know what another translator, John Oliver Simon, reports, that black stone over white stone refers to a prehistoric board game found in the ruins of Pachacamac southeast of Lima, and black stone over white is the move of death. Vallejo, whose grandmothers were indigenous Chimú Indians, would know the game. While it is a violent poem in which the speaker is beaten, it is also a mysterious poem in which the speaker "has put his upper arm bones on wrong." The poet is not about to sentimentalize. The poem ends not on the speaker, but rather on the surprising witnesses to his death:

César Vallejo is dead. Everyone beat him
although he never does anything to them;
they beat him hard with a stick and hard also

with a rope. These are the witnesses:
the Thursdays, and the bones of my arms,
the solitude, and the rain, and the roads . . .

Vallejo chooses not to return to the mystery of the title, nor to elaborate on the cause of his demise, nor to reveal the meaning of life, nor even to enlist Paris, the city in which he predicts he will live his last day. No, the poem's ending is intentionally sidelined by ellipsis.

I fear that many contemporary poems hesitate to travel inward, or circuitously, to see where connotative messages lead. With their situations in the way, they may have many words, but not many worlds; they prefer to report, defend, and review. A great poem, in revealing human weakness or strength, never advances its argument, sound, song, tale, list or meditation merely for the record. I suggest that the best poets intuitively work away from their indulgences, their perfected habits, and this humility morphs cultural, political, and spiritual experiences into lines that make reality extraordinary. A poem should aspire to a version almost too good to be true, almost as if it never happened.

Tie Up Your Dinghy & Help Me

1. Surrealism, Get Super-real!

I promise this will barely even twist your nipple . . .
This is just saying things like a ringer . . .
Look, this is a couple of sentences that make some demands on the meat in your
*   skull . . .*
Don't be entertained!

That's the opening of "Six Short Poems," by Chesley Minnis. And this is a stanza from her poem "Art: Three Women":

I don't like to be bored. I love to be bored.
It's also time to be terrific.
I couldn't live without being so terrific.
Now give me your drama,
like little bits of flesh among the diamonds.

Or consider these lines, from her book *Baby, I Don't Care*:

"Baby, it's so sexy to think.
Why don't you try it?" she says.
And: "Try not to talk when you're sober, darling."
She coos, "You're so handsome it's a shame.
It makes me want to murder some pigeons."

Painful, witty, satiric, what is it?

Surrealism, the famous twentieth-century movement, encouraged automatic writing and wild imaginings that broke realism into a thousand puzzle pieces, swept some out, and rearranged language indiscriminately, on purpose. The rule was: no rules. A century later, it can be fun, sloppy, sparkling and imaginative. But let's get super-real. Outlandish, sometimes infantile, inventions show up in contemporary poetry. Don't skip ahead, looking for trashed samples, that's not my game, although it is one of surrealism's, in the sense stated in André Breton's 1924 manifesto, bemoaning that "our mind scarcely dares express itself" and insisting that surrealism is the only true technique in poetry. Putting down writing that is not utterly devoid of reason, he makes the case for surrealism by defining it as psychic automatism:

> Surrealism, n.,: Psychic automatism in its pure state, by which one proposes to express—verbally, by means of the written word, or in any other manner—the actual functioning of thought. Dictated by the thought, in the absence of any control exercised by reason, exempt from any aesthetic or moral concern.

One can hear the counterargument that poetry is dictated by aesthetic or moral concerns. It is a raging debate, and the ethicists, as the twenty-first century advances, lead the day. Identity politics in poetry disavows the right to imaginatively enter—and thereby possibly exploit in a patronizing, colonialist way—any culture not one's own. But contemporary poems need not devolve into endless identity victim-narratives or absurd flights of fanciful imagery. At the extremes, these ideals extract the worst in their respective poetries.

What attracted a poet like Odysseas Elytis to surrealism, as Sam Hamill put it some years after serving as editor to Olga Broumas's gorgeous Elytis translations, *What I Love*, "was not its revolutionary rejection of traditional versification nor its stream of consciousness technique, but its faith in intuition. . . . Imagination is accepted as being just as 'real' as the temporal physical world."

Super-real images function in a lexicon of possible scenarios between pure invention and realism. When Minnis's speaker wants to "murder some pigeons," what is that tone? Excess, calumny, comedy? The category of the possible, if unlikely or uncanny, provides a lifeline to a world that readers share and also a critique of that world. A poem is a world because it is many worlds. We might ask of the surreal contribution in a poem if it offers something to adjudicate, to consider, or is it entertainment? A clever writer can invent a wild image in a poem, one with its implied or asserted exclamation point. But it can flatten the world into two dimensions, like entertainment on a screen. How might we serve identity-sensitive poems and also give integrity to the flimsiest exuberances? Super-real acts, I suggest, with components of sense and anarchy, may avoid both the guest who attends the party to lecture everyone, and the guest who shows up drunk.

2. The Problem with Women

It's worth mentioning at this juncture that most puerile representations of surrealism can be traced back to a naive and chauvinistic tone in its founder's official announcement. In manifestos of 1924 and 1929, André Breton laid the foundation for an infamous misogyny: "The problem of woman is the most marvellous and disturbing problem in all the world." In revering them as muses, women got erased as artists, thinkers, and activists. Chelsey Minnis has given contemporary surrealism a welcome female speaker. She's joined by the publication of *The Milk Bowl of Feathers* a few years ago, "a new collection of surrealist writers [focusing] on women authors," according to Joseph Nechvatal, in *Hyperallergic*. But even his positive review describes the anthology's caption as an exaggeration: "Though the subtitle of the book, *Essential Surrealist Writings*, is hyperbolic and somewhat misleading, *The Milk Bowl of Feathers* is a decisive *addition* to the Surrealist English library." Hardly of the essence, and late to the game?

Nechvatal does make the important judgment: "These women's contributions captivatingly crack the wall of Surrealist phallocracy principally erected from André Breton's misogyny. Breton viewed every Surrealist woman as a *femme enfant* who helped provide the male artists' access to the ingenuous unconscious." I bet you have not heard (yet) of many of these women or thought of them as specific to surrealist poetry: Dora Maar, Joyce Mansour, Elsa von Freytag-Loringhoven, Claude Cahun, Leonora Carrington, Mina Loy, Alice Rahon, Gisèle Prassinos, Kay Sage, Meret Oppenheim, and Léona Delcourt (aka Nadja). Is Chelsey Minnis, at her most extravagant, a last hurrah of a movement out of sync with our time, calling poetry, in *Baby, I Don't Care*, "a shimmer like flushing sequins down the toilet"?

3. What Fun!

In support of his herald of the surreal, Breton quotes a typical fanfaronade from poet Louis Aragon:

> During a short break in the party, as the players were gathering around a bowl of flaming punch, I asked a tree if it still had its red ribbon.

What fun! The punchbowl in flames, a tree queried about its decorative ribbon. It feels alive, awake. A tree is addressed with mock or, at most, passing concern. It's all very amusing. The fragment oozes charm. But reading into Aragon's work reveals an undercurrent of agony. Compare "flaming punch" to his "flaming city" in this fragment from the battlelines of the French port city where Allied forces were attempting to evacuate, "Night at Dunkirk":

. . . I'll cry I'll cry in the flaming city
To shake the somnambulists from the roofs

I'll cry forth my love as in the morning
Early the grinder passed crying Knives Knives

I'll cry I'll cry Eyes that I love where are
You O where are you where my lark my gull

I'll cry I'll cry louder than cry the shells
Louder than the wounded and the drunk

Lives are not typically as charmed as their author's charmed projects, and Aragon's certainly wasn't. He discovers a family secret at age nineteen, when he's about to go to war, and only because no one thinks he will return: His father had seduced a seventeen-year-old, when he was nearly fifty, and abandoned her and also his son. Aragon was raised by his mother and maternal grandmother, believing them to be his sister and foster mother.

Eventually, Louis, a Jew, ends up on a list of forbidden authors in Vichy France. His surrealism is closely tied to resistance work underground and childhood trauma. Loss, confusion, and violence, framed jocularly and mysteriously, support his flamboyant literary style. While no psychological or cultural situation entirely explains a poet's inclinations or decisions in art, I only suggest that Aragon's impressive imagination is deeply embedded in reality: As he says, "I am caught in a net of falling stars/ Like a sailor who dies at sea in the middle of August."

Surrealism, impressive in itself, is only a device. But if it is *for* something, in service of a layered awareness and conscience, it is a cubist lens on that viscera. We get to see the world torqued open, not to confirm its meaninglessness, but to free ourselves from convention and subjugation. Surrealism was never meant to be a game; it serves to empower. Where is its place in a twenty-first century in which the contemporary American version tends toward the random or childish, having the effect of excluding or underestimating its audience? American poets need to drop the unhinged poem that has lost its associations and connotations, its mysterious trails, as George Trakl puts it, "as darkening thunder drives over the hill." Or, put another way, Trakl also wrote, "I drank the silence of God out of the stream in the trees." The poem continues:

Cold metal walks on my forehead.
Spiders search for my heart.
It is a light that goes out in my mouth.

The poet's sphere is an emotional place. Poetry at its best is spirited, tracking the senses and consciousness. Do you fear that I will mention beauty next? Well, yes, discernment is what is beautiful about truth. In Robert Bly and James Wright's excellent translations, we hear the young Trakl's agony. He will be dead of an overdose of drugs, war, and melancholy before he's 28.

4. A Six-Pack of Corona

It's easy to send a walrus for a beer in a poem in Tucson, Arizona, where craft breweries line the downtown. A walrus might be seen daydreaming over *Barrio Blonde*, *Nightwater Black*, *The Way of the Coyote Pale Ale*, or *Lolo's Brown* while waiting for a friend or a date, when suddenly a monsoon floods the patio. It's also easy to strap a walrus into a spaceship or onto a flying anthill, and never toward a church, with its grandmother counting a stack of money. I suppose I could go on with this silliness. The general tendency has been to bloat the surreal. Confidently, these creations are in no need of logic. But like shaken beer, surrealism explodes its container. American poets have spent decades stomaching deadpan narrations, one-dimensional characters, and puzzling alienations, a surplus of wonders and terrors. The danger now, if we abandon the surreal for the real, is that we have a similar problem—we become so explicit as to become inaccessible to each another.

Too much subjectivity can be exclusive, may stifle what poet Reginald Shepherd, and Emily Dickinson before him, called, "being no one at all":

> I have always intensely disliked what I call identity poetics. . . . That has always seemed to me a form of self-imprisonment, neglecting or even negating the possibilities poetry offers not just of being someone else, anyone and/or everyone else, but of being no one at all, of existing (if only for a moment) outside the shackles of identity and definition. Ideally, one writes poetry out of what one doesn't know, as an act of exploration.

The most precarious place from which to draw one's creative inspiration is a land of dreams and responsibilities. To represent that vulnerability, while confronting the impossibility of representation, is a paradox readymade for poetry.

5. Lamb Innards

Before my encounter with Federico García Lorca, I thought of love as omnivorous and sensual, like the heat of the summer sun. In life and art, I was inexperienced, vague, and romantic, and as I lay around reading under that sun, my homosexuality, like Lorca's, was visibly hidden by the overgrown limbs of my family tree. I was the permitted "tomboy," a popular lesbian camouflage losing its luster past childhood. When I studied Lorca's fantasia of romantic and surreal imagery, it seemed painfully accompanied by hiddenness, also death and darkness. His poetry was resonant with my anxieties about "coming out" in an antagonistic setting on the page or promenade, so I was open to its strange figures.

As a historian and a preservationist of culture, Lorca's quest for identity was entwined with the reading of a forbidding social landscape. Despite or because of his "outsiderness," his poems interrogate experience and become an experience in themselves. He describes his most popular collection, *Romancero Gitano* (*Gypsy Ballads*), as a "carved altar piece [of Andalusia's] gypsies, horses, archangels, planets, its Jewish and Roman breezes, rivers, crimes, the everyday touch of the smuggler and the celestial note of the naked children of Córdoba. A book that hardly expresses visible Andalusia at all, but where the hidden Andalusia trembles." When he writes, "Black horses and sinister people travel the deep roads of the guitar," we feel the exquisite pressure of fresh language, as well as the dangerous pressure of the law, on the Roma (formerly, "Gypsy") community he adores.

Recently, Sarah Arvio brings us *Poet in Spain* (Knopf, 2017), which includes her Lorca translation of a scrap of unfinished sonnet, a draft on thin paper from the Hotel Victoria in Valencia:

Oh hotel bed oh this sweet bed
Oh sheet of whitenesses and dew
Hum of your body with my body
Cave of cotton flame and shadow

Oh double lyre that my love branches
around your thighs of fire and cold white nard
Oh tipping raft—oh bright river—
now a branch and now a nightingale

Following three sentimental opening lines, Lorca leaps into the surreal without warning. Inventive personifications and startling juxtapositions crackle with passion. His surreal nouns, "cave of cotton flame and shadow," surprise us with elemental, abstract shape. The unusual image comes alive in an environment of a river, a branch, the dew, a hotel, and ultimately, love itself. The earthy descriptors are no mere accessories, but rather a ground for extravagant archetypal effects. Deep into the fantasia, "around your thighs of fire and cold white nard" sounds grandiose, as well as taut and nervous, especially with *nardo's* hard "n" and "d." But it is far from a capricious choice.

White nard isn't any roadside weed, merely commandeered for its iron sound in the poem, but rather is an ancient, aromatic plant with a musky scent, grown in Nepal's Himalayas, China, India, Syria, and along the western slope of the Hindu Kush. Found at especially high altitude, it yields an ancient perfume and medicine that made its way along the ancient Silk Road to Europe. Its perfume stood for centuries as an evocation of the aroma of the lost Garden of Eden. Lorca would have been very familiar with it, if not familiar with nard's English slang meaning of "balls" or bravado, from "nads," a shortened form of gonads. I can't help but think he'd be amused by that pun, while certainly aware of the flower's association with self-sacrifice, humility, and faith in the Hispanic iconographic tradition, where "Joseph is depicted with a branch of spikenard in his hand." Lorca was steeped in Catholic pageantry, and also aware of spikenard's use in recipes, as he was often served food derived from his homeland's Moorish occupation. Born into a relatively wealthy family, he may have eaten a servant's Andalusian chicken sausage, prepared like this one from *An Anonymous Andalusian Cookbook of the 13th Century*, translated by Charles Perry:

> If it is tender, take the flesh of the breast of the hen or partridge or the flesh of the thighs and grind it up very vigorously, and remove the tendons and grind with the meat almonds, walnuts, and pine nuts until completely mixed, throw in pepper, caraway, cinnamon, spikenard, in the required quantity, a little honey and eggs, beat all together until it becomes one substance, then make with this what looks like an "usba" made of lamb innards and put it in a lamb skin or sheep skin and put it on a heated skewer and cook slowly over a fire of hot coals until it is browned, then remove it and eat it, if you wish with murri and if you wish with mustard, if God so wills.

Nard in skewered lambsacks—it's nearly surreal. Coals, honey, animal flesh—Lorca was surrounded by essences and symbols born of local plants, metals, jewels, horses, widows, knives and matadors. Inhabited by close families, Andalusia was a hot, dry, elemental landscape with a thin membrane between materiality and metaphor.

Liz Henry, another Lorca translator, elaborates on the poet's choice of *nardo* in the more serious context of a sexy, morbid, funeral splendor, a heavy overpowering incense with erotic notes and religious undertones for wakes and funerals. It's no surprise that the plant blossoms at night and is associated with myth and magic. Lorca's fire, flames, whiteness, and shadow, spirited and ancestral elements, flourish alongside, and because of, the touchstones of emotion in his poem. The surrealism is physical, terrifying, and haunted, what Arvio refers to as "a wild, innate, local surrealism . . . of lemon groves and bandits on black horses." Lorca's diction is never arbitrary or casual. Here is another moment for the white nard plant, the opening of "Ballad of the Moon Moon":

Moon came to the forge
in her petticoat of nard
The boy looks and looks
the boy looks at the Moon
In the turbulent air
Moon lifts up her arms
showing—pure and sexy—
her beaten-tin breasts

The erotic scene contains "turbulent air" and "beaten-tin," a skein of danger and of death, with a petticoat of funereal nard. Lorca writes, "Everywhere else, death is an end. Death comes, and they draw the curtains. Not in Spain. In Spain they open them. Many Spaniards live indoors until the day they die and are taken out into the sunlight. In Spain the dead are more alive than the dead in any other country in the world." Seemingly impossible figures of nightmare and reality blend seamlessly because they are rooted in folklore. Such a clear connection to the past paradoxically affords Lorca a vision of the future. It is well known that Lorca predicted his own murder near a spring in an olive grove.

6. Barbies

The tough and comic way in which Chelsey Minnis approaches relation-ships in poems suggests that she's trained to confront disaster because she's a woman. She's ducking and then is in your face, nimble as a pugi-list. In reviewing Minnis's poems in "Riot Girl," Sandra Simonds refers to Joyelle McSweeney's point that Minnis's poems create "a space for nego-tiating agency and autonomy in a world where erasure is the historical norm for female poets." She cares to commit, at crucial moments in a poem, to reality. Her poems are not fun all the way in. The bubbly surface is dangerously volcanic.

More than is obvious at first eruption, Chelsey Minnis's sarcasm serves her political and cultural critique of these often fascist times. Minnis's bravado staves off anxiety and loss. We are, as she says, "little bits of flesh among the diamonds." And yet, if poems as fabulously fun and creative as Chelsey Minnis's still leave some readers to wonder if the speaker is simply a wise-ass, what does this bode for the future of the wild and irra-tional in poems? They may indeed wonder if Minnis's soul is exclaiming from a maelstrom, or if her compositions are a ruse, an *amuse-bouche*, teasing, rich, after which, no main course? (No "*usba* of lamb innards"?) Have contemporary writers cheapened a movement formerly rooted in a shared history, a communal unconscious? Are we interested merely in airy trifles? No less a fantasist than Wallace Stevens warns us, through Coleridge, that some visions are "fanciful," not creative or original, but borrowed:

> Fancy, then, is an exercise of selection from among objects already supplied by association, a selection made for purposes which are not then and therein being shaped but have been already fixed.

To me, Minnis's poems read as political barbs ("barbies," my cheap pun, see, it's easy) against normative behavior. Is the speaker cynical? ironic? Do those tones cheapen poetry? I find them flimsy covers for sharp talk that is quite subversive. The sensationalized lines tease convention:

This is the time to be congenial but I can't make it.
I'm the type who never likes your type.
Don't you see?
We're filthy in love.
Let's get some rice thrown on us.
  (From "Art: Three Women")

7. Angel Dust

Wallace Stevens expresses his literary anxieties in "The Noble Rider and the Sound of Words": "The imagination loses vitality as it ceases to adhere to what is real." Let's remember who Stevens's "necessary angel" is. It is not the angel of the imagination, whom we might expect from the often remote Stevens, but rather the angel of reality. Steven's Hegelian reading of reality, where the world is a reflection of the mind, provides the groundwork for the poet as noble rider, a figure who lives uncommonly in a common world. Stevens thinks of Cervantes's Don Quixote as the quintessential figure. Battered and maligned for his visions, unfortunately the Don dies of suffering the extremes of both reality and the imagination—his reality becomes too real, stripped of excitement and amusement, and his imaginings make him light-headed, multiplying figures and meanings and worlds until they dissipate into thin air. All his fabulous adventures end as they must, in stark, cold reality. With bravery, courtesy, and honor forsworn, our man—for he surely belongs in our embrace—dies in his own bed of a fever.

Does a reckoning happen in art when the contributions from the real and the imagined fall out of balance? Stevens, who works to create a real world out of his visions, nevertheless wrote, in 1936, that "in the presence of extraordinary actuality, consciousness takes the place of the imagination." The distressed present acutely focuses all our attention. Susan Briante's book *Defacing the Monument* speaks directly to the artist's responsibility in our time, and indirectly to the challenges of agency and imagination in art. Hers is a work of creative nonfiction—a category that did not exist during Stevens's lifetime—a bracing, post-lyrical meditation on authority that gathers the poet, memoirist, collagist, journalist, and historian into herself to create a text. Her lyrical publication takes its place among the politically active books by poets of the last century who combined the hybridity of free associations with "extraordinary actuality." Briante quotes Stevens: "Stevens explained that the Depression had focused everyone's attention 'in the direction of reality, that is to say in the direction of fact.'" Briante's ideal citizen, the activist, confronts the artist, a flawed and virtuous figure:

> The pen is not a metaphor for giving tools. A tool is the flag hung over the water barrel or the coordinates of the water barrel written into the code and transmitted to the migrant's phone or the poem that helped the migrant locate the north star.

Defacing the Monument presents local history, family, and reverie in a lyrical montage centered around migrants and migration. Briante joins last century's Adrienne Rich, Muriel Rukeyser, and William Carlos Williams, and contemporary guides Claudia Rankine and Maggie Nelson, none of whom, like Briante, are associated with the surreal, but who nevertheless exemplify the best of its rejection of historical "norms." Ingrid Pfeiffer, curator of the exhibition *Fantastic Women: Surreal Worlds from Meret Oppenheim to Frida Kahlo*, asserts that, despite surrealism relegating women to the old whores-or-saints categories, inadvertently the surrealist movement "in many ways strikes as decidedly 'feminine,' since it rejected all traditionally masculine, patriarchal, and imperialist structures."

At inception, the movement had to do with politics, with the desire to subvert authority. Rooted in a Europe of a hundred years ago, it was a response to rational writing. To tap the unconscious was to break from conformity into imaginative revelations, and not where romanticism posited them to be found, in nature, but rather in the street. The movement spoke to the reader at a visceral level, not simply as escapist entertainment. It is a sad and ironic state of North American poetic affairs that the techniques that were to liberate us from realism often have turned slapstick and absurd. Automatic writing, non sequiturs, palindromes, echo poems, cut-ups, and word lists perform, Pow! Pow! Pow!, throwing jabs indiscriminately, punching the air until the poem falls to earth, collapsing on a whim.

8. Surrealism, Wake Up! It's Tomorrow

Let's get super-real. My title, "Tie Up Your Dinghy & Help Me," is glib. Smooth, a little insincere, and worse, it assumes the reader is familiar with the specialty word "dinghy," a small boat often in service as a lifeboat, commonly hitched to the sides of yachts. And what could be worse than associating poetry with yachts. Furthermore, the zingy title avails itself of the rhym-y "dinghy"/"help me," so as to allow a minor achievement in music to cover the meaning's potential political problems. What little immediate charm is granted by the imperative form and a breezy, New York-school tone gets complicated, possibly doomed, by the effete world of yachts. Nobody wants to deploy rich people; ironizing them takes valuable time. The unfortunate acoustic pun of dinghy with "ding-dong," a foolish person, compounds the trouble. Maybe the plea, "Help me," has enough humility for the reader to endure these self-inflicted wounds.

But why fuss, you might ask, about a throwaway title that meant no harm and is, after all, kind of pleasant? Am I attracted to surrealism as to a bad relationship? My claim that you have a dinghy, which you might set aside to help me, assigns you property and potentially leisure you may ill afford. The imposition of my conjured world on you puts you at my disposal. Or maybe it's merely cartoon-y and gratuitous. At its best, surrealism is American poetry's inherited, free experiment, and, with some care and resistance, it works very seriously to undermine norms. What subversion, if any, was my title after? It seems rather fanciful and carefree, even careless. I suppose I would rather quote my own slippage into weightless figures than anybody else's. It's easy to dilute a historically liberating movement.

By the late twentieth century, John Ashbery is teaching us to adore phenomenology and expressionism, and, combined with self-reflection, to make thrilling compositional romps. Hey, what a great party, following the American surrealists as they ironized with book titles such as *Classic Ballroom Dances* (Charles Simic), *Riven Doggeries* (James Tate), or *Elegy on a Toy Piano* (Dean Young). Meanwhile, I can't remember a line that sounded like terrific fun in Adrienne Rich or Audre Lorde, two of the more prominent women writers sharing Ashbery's era. They are not *performing*. They didn't have time to fool around, so they didn't mess with its frame. The times had already messed with them.

What time is it now?

Given the desperateness of the actual world, there is little patience for school buses smoking cigars or loaves of rye bread kissing. Imagery—poets have options. When poets cannily amuse themselves, they avoid a shadow going across a wall, a tire blown out by a rifle on a roof. Unless we select effects, however strained or phantasmagoric, that speak to shared concerns, the art form will wither.

Awe is different from glee. Does a reader prefer to be giddy, or to be changed? I'm guided by Claudia Rankine's remark that "the psyche holds a trauma that seems a greater violence than anything the physical body can hold. I am held by those moments. When the circumstance of the body becomes treated like the stunts of the body, the psyche is at an even further remove from healing."

9. More than Two Advil

Regarding bodies and trauma, Guillaume Apollinaire is an interesting case. Before he put himself in physical danger, he made twentieth-century poetry dangerous by removing the mind's resting places in his first book, *Alcool* (*Alcohol*), in one gesture impulsively taking out all punctuation the night before its publication, allowing it to flow like time itself. This visionary 1913 aesthetic decision is still current over a century later. Then suddenly, at age thirty-five, he volunteered for war, sending strange poems of praise home.

From military training camp, he wrote, "I love art so much, I have joined the artillery" ("J'aime tellement l'art, j'ai rejoint l'artillerie"), one of many puns and non sequiturs that have created countless imitators, unable to match his strange amalgam of charm, suffering, and beauty. In the classic, casually titled "The Pretty Redhead," we find the speaker, who has been wounded on a battlefield, getting his head trepanned under chloroform. And yet, the unpunctuated tone is strangely exhilarating:

We who seek adventure everywhere

We are not your enemies
We want to give you vast and strange territories
Where flowering mystery offers itself to anyone who wishes to gather it

But did he aggrandize brutality and terror in troubling ways? He sent this poem of an April night in a war zone back to friends in Paris:

Hear our shells sing
Their deep purple love hailed by our men going to die

The wet springtime the night light the attack

It's raining my soul it's raining but it's raining dead eyes

Ulysses how many days to get back to Ithaca

Lie down in the straw and dream a fine remorse
Which as a pure effect of art is aphrodisiac

Tony Hoagland unsuspectedly spells out the problem with Apollinaire's glorification of war in a review praising "imaginative wildness." Apollinaire's war poems

> challenge the reader who would segregate ethical understanding and imaginative wildness. These poems, however, are insistently astonishing—never jaded and, in fact, always wholesome. They exemplify the unquenchable capacity of the human imagination, which roams outside prescribed boundaries and finds delight and humor even in the middle of suffering.

And presto, surrealism's embrace of violence, in the name of wonder, becomes part of the American postmodernist poet's vernacular, especially untoward if the writer has had the privilege of being raised in relative safety. Wham! You're dead. Bam! But wait, is it fake blood? Is it fresh blood, made phosphorescent?

Apollinaire's many poems are virtuoso performances in the frenzy of soldiering and adventuring, and they range from bloody to loving. Before he ever goes off to love or war, he works as a secretary by day and by night writes sci-fi and porn. Critic Donald Lyons has called him "jovial, lewd, manic, and charismatic." His "swashbuckling" spirit, a term derived from swaggering swordsmen and daredevil adventurers, owes much to the mythology around the tradesmen who plied the ancient Silk Road. These iconic drivers traveled not only across scorching deserts but along the frozen passes of the Pamir Mountains astride the venerable camel. Apollinaire references the route from Persia to the silk factories of Lyon, France in "Tree,"

Don't abandon me among this crowd of women at the market
Isfahan made a sky of blue enameled tiles
And I go up with you a road around Lyon

Apollinaire's affection for mythic figures—adventurer and beast—survives in the composer Francis Poulenc's first song cycle, based on Apollinaire's first book, *Le Bestiaire*, which Poulenc composed on the piano at a local elementary school while serving as a typist at the Ministry of Aviation during the war. One of my favorite of these short ditties regards one Don Pedro, heroic Portuguese soldier who set off with twelve companions mounted on four camels—improvisatory, if not luxurious—to visit the seven regions of the world, which journey involved winning battles and receiving titles from nobles. Don Pedro fought valiantly well into his fifties, dying in an otherwise successful major battle near Lisbon, by the creek of Alfarrobeira, immortalized by Apollinaire in "The Dromedary," which succinctly runs:

With his four dromedaries
Don Pedro d'Alfaroubeira
Roamed the world and admired it.
He did what I would like to do
If I had four dromedaries too.

This sweet homage to the glories of exploring and warring forecasts the ease with which Apollinaire later exaggerates or roseates. But his most memorable surrealist poems saturate heightened action in natural color and feeling, careful to avoid figures so exclusive as to omit or betray us. Rather, they act in unison with our natural emblems, among them night, day, earth, and shadow, images such as we find in Ocean Vuong's strange, personal poem "DetoNation," aptly re-capitalized for maximum political effect. The poem opens on the end of a joke:

There's a joke that ends with—huh?
It's the bomb saying here is your father.

Now here is your father inside
your lungs. Look how lighter

the earth is—afterward.
To even write the word father

is to carve a portion of the day
out of a bomb-bright page.

10. What Dwells in the Almond

One cannot approach the surreal and trauma in poetry without coming face to face with Paul Celan. He is the supreme navigator of the irrational depths of the psyche. His education in surrealist practice involved translating Paul Eluard, Robert Desnos, and others, but Celan's poetry is an experience in semantic dislocation and sensory impression like no one else's. He detonates narrative in favor of a code or cipher of emotion. Celan's need for neologisms and his recast of elemental language come from excavating primordial, as much as European, history. Here, in Michael Hamburger's translation, is the paradoxical opening of Celan's "Mandorla," referencing the almond-shaped aureole surrounding an iconographic figure, an image both hollow and hallowed:

In the almond—what dwells in the almond?
Nothing.
What dwells in the almond is Nothing.
There it dwells and dwells.

I don't speak German, and even if you do not, to hear Celan reading this poem is to hear music from the small cathedral of the almond, deep into magical, existential, and ordinary time. Moments magnified, contracted, and repeated
(https://www.youtube.com/watch?v=X31Dp_7tVG8).

On the other side of the globe, a similar mythmaking power also appears around the mid-twentieth century in the unheralded literary genre of the Native American autobiography, which saw *Black Elk Speaks* (1932) and *Sun Chief* (1942) explore magic, metaphor, and symbol. "Crazy Horse dreamed and went into the world where there is nothing but the spirits of all things. That is the real world that is behind this one," Black Elk wrote. He continues, "Perhaps you have noticed that even in the slightest breeze you can hear the voice of the cottonwood tree." This dreamy shape-shifting is rooted and spiritual, and it reminds me of Lorca's "hidden Andalusia." The extrasensual experience carries on in contemporary anthropomorphic Native poems like Joy Harjo's "For Calling the Spirit Back from Wandering the Earth in its Human Feet," in which the poem itself, a mostly declarative list, admonishes, "Watch your mind. Without training it might run away and leave / your heart for the immense human feast set by the thieves of time." The Native tradition at its most aware of myth and memory offers a super-real adventure of value, of ritual and political intent, rather than one of frivolity or simplicity.

11. Fuck the Astronauts

The best surrealist poems recognize a connection from mythology to history. The poem that lapses into purely absurdist territory sometimes gets into morally ambiguous places. Consider both the opening and closing of James Tate's "Fuck the Astronauts":

Eventually we must combine nightmares
an angel smoking a cigarette on the steps
of the last national bank, said to me.
I put her out with my thumb. I don't need that
cheap talk I've got my own problems.
It was sad, exciting, and horrible.
It was exciting, horrible, and sad.
It was horrible, sad, and exciting.
It was inviting, mad, and deplorable.
It was adorable, glad, and enticing.
. . .

I am the hashish pinball machine
that rapes a piano.

Tate is one of our most brilliant surrealists, devastatingly funny, and also remarkably in touch with human frailty. The opening, "Eventually we must combine nightmares," goes on to be funny, talky, crazy, and dark. Critic Richard Wirick has expressed what I ordinarily appreciate about the people in Tate's poems: "They are stick figures, but their language . . . gives them the fullness of crushed spirits." But "Fuck the Astronauts" crosses beyond the absurd into evil, ending on a rape. Tate's rape of a piano is gratuitously violent and offensive. It ignores Claudia Rankine's concerns for the human psyche. The anthropomorphized piano is a joke too far. The best Tate poems accomplish what the best of John Ashbery poems could, and cared to, do—have an ethical sensibility. Among many conflated worlds, among so many subjectivities and non sequiturs, time's impress on Ashbery's pilgrimage through language is duly noted by Tate with an insouciant wink, and most often Tate's knowing gestures respect us.

Similar to Wallace Stevens and Ashbery, Tate's sensualist's touch more often presses to reconnect with the life of ideas, the life of the mind. Tate's poems are seldom corrosive on the human spirit. His best work is inventive, personal, social, and connotative (with the pun on his name, thx, surrealism, always correcting for scholarly pretension). This is the ending of "The Government Lake":

A man walked up behind me and said, "This government lake is
off-limits to the public. You'll have to leave." I said,
"I didn't know it was a government lake. Why should it be
off-limits?" He said, "I'm sorry. You'll have to leave."
"I don't even know where I am," I said. "You'll still have
to leave," he said. "What about that man out there?" I said,
pointing to the tire. "He's dead," he said. "No, he's not.
I just saw him move his arm," I said. He removed his pistol from
his holster and fired a shot. "Now he's dead," he said.

The gallows humor would be slapstick funny if it weren't damning social commentary. This exchange could be in Briante's *Defacing the Mon-*

ument, part of her moving report of the callous disregard for life at the border of the United States and Mexico. Her text includes a student's confrontation with border police who were invited into her classroom, the same authorities who had slashed water bottles and confiscated shoes from people crossing the spiky landscape. Reality and empathy force Briante to describe barbed wire, border walls, police brutality—statistics and depictions in a conversation with James Agee's *Let Us Now Praise Famous Men*, on the lives of tenant farmers harassed and forgotten during the Depression.

Reality asks what the artistic imagination is for. It's a better question than asking what does art mean. Agee's answer is embedded in plans he made to expand his project, which, though never written, speaks to his poetic nature, for he wanted to make "an independent inquiry into certain normal predicaments of human divinity." Although Agee only ever wrote one book of poems, *Permit Me Voyage*, he never abandoned his passion for the otherworldliness of reality. But he avoided creative figures conjured for pleasure alone. Do we really want to be high on that drug, stripped of inhibitions and also conscience? For then, who are we? What will we have created?

12. Hello, Transgressor

Wallace Stevens's sense of the demands on language caused by an "extraordinary actuality" surfaces for another poet, Akilah Oliver, some fifty years after Stevens's difficult reckoning with the Depression and World War II. Oliver contracts diction and syntax under the pressure of the incomprehensible in her poem "In Aporia," which begins with a familiar surrealist tool, a pun. "Aporia" sounds like "Peoria," a specific locale, while an "aporia" is a logical disjunction in a text, puzzle, or impasse. Oliver shifts the locus from Beckett's theater of the absurd to the street, employing metaphor and metonym, the imagined and real. Here is an excerpt:

hello transgressor, you've come to collect utilitarian debts, humbling

narrative space. Give me a condition and wheatgrass,

I his body is disintegrating, I his body is ossification. Death by habit

radius, yeah yeah.

I his body can't refuse this summons. I can't get out

this fucking room. Tell me something different about torture

dear Trickster.

Further along,

I his body keeps thinking someone will come along, touch me.

As like human. Or lima bean.

Where Chelsey Minnis relies on the sarcastic and gnomic, and is declarative and discursive, Oliver's grammar is disjunctive, but serious emotional needs guide both poets. While "lima bean" may seem arbitrary here, it stands in for our fragile, minimized condition. Oliver could be writing about herself in speaking about poet Anne Waldman's poetics:

> So I also think of Anne's work in terms of the artist as warrior, or as cultural worker. . . . How do you do that without desecrating, without destroying, without becoming the destructiveness that we associate with the militaristic sense of war? What comes to mind with the idea of artist as warrior is that the artist shape-shifts, that the artist is able to occupy multiple sites, not necessarily simultaneously, but able to occupy multiple sites.

When the pressures on truth become too great or too dull, poets are called upon to recalibrate surrealism and reality. I accidently typed "realty"—proof again that the unconscious is a busy, funny, disruptive place. But, "Cuidado, cuidado, cuidado," "Careful, careful, careful," as Lorca said, "no es sueño la vida." Life is not a dream.

13. Window Washing

The composer John Cage, one of the brilliant theorists of the avant-garde, was not above washing the walls of the Brooklyn YWCA when he arrived in New York. He had a lot of ideas about art but loved the "noise" of things. In his musical compositions and his writing, he seems to hear the cosmos giggling. He tells the story of his first day in the city with such élan, it is easy to forget he is destitute:

> When Xenia and I came to New York from Chicago, we arrived in the bus station with about twenty-five cents. We were expecting to stay for a while with Peggy Guggenheim and Max Ernst. Max Ernst had met us in Chicago and had said, "Whenever you come to New York, come and stay with us. We have a big house on the East River." I went to the phone booth in the bus station, put in a nickel, and dialed. Max Ernst answered. He didn't recognize my voice. Finally he said, "Are you thirsty?" I said, "Yes." He said, "Well, come over tomorrow for cocktails." I went back to Xenia and told her what had happened. She said, "Call him back. We have everything to gain and nothing to lose." I did. He said, "Oh, it's you. We've been waiting for you for weeks. Your room's ready. Come right over."

Cage's disarming sense of humor and trust in a quirky universe equipped him for further adventures in the arts. What began as a fascination with collages, stream of consciousness writing, and Dada absurdist works became an imperative to give up creative control, even the unconscious automatic writing that animated surrealist projects. As a composer, in opening the mind to more than itself, he opened the doors of the concert hall to let in the random sounds of the neighborhood. And of course, this is the guy who famously wrote a piece to last four minutes and thirty-three seconds for any combination of instruments, provided the performers not play them.

Cage's work is designed to wake us up to the very life we're living by getting our minds out of the way. Yet he admitted that he fiddled with his creations, even as he trusted chance. Perhaps artists such as Akilah Oliver and John Cage are both disruptive of the merely existent or the merely fanciful. Oliver values the warrior-poet, and Cage would prefer to remove the composer from all ego intention. Both makers are aware, as

Stevens cautions, "It is not that there is a new imagination but that there is a new reality." Oliver and Cage both convince me that any "super-real" poetic space reveals, rather than obscures, consciousness and conscience. As John Cage wrote, in *Silence*, "A sound accomplishes nothing; without it life would not last out the instant."

A poem acknowledges an almond is never just an almond, but it is an almond. That inclusivity frees us, at no one else's expense, nor our own, and tethers us to earth. Super-realistic figures in a poem blow open real windows of perception with otherworldly force. I find it beautiful that some images are not larger than life but announce that life is large.

Fantasia on Paul Klee in Tunisia

1.

In April of 1914, it went largely unnoticed that the painter Paul Klee spent two weeks in Tunisia. Klee was an inquisitive tourist, astonished, to his great pleasure and education, by a brightly lit North Africa. It was to have a huge effect on his previously lackadaisical sense of hue and proportion in his paintings. Blocks of dazzling structures of color and light formed geometric shapes and illusions in the new watercolors he made. Pastels and black lines built drapes of contrasting colorscapes. His watercolors model the whimsy and unity of nature, but they sign and pattern like dreams. Suddenly, a world opened, as he put it, to "abstraction, with memories."

Klee took to intertwining the visual and verbal with hieroglyphs and squiggles. Among trails of markings, he laced searing orange backgrounds with domes, decorated windows, cacti gardens, bushes, and reeds, all of which formed, he wrote in his diaries, "a beautiful rhythm of patches." He made thirty-five such watercolors and fifteen drawings in brilliant tints inspired by the scorching sun. The experiments sacrificed the illusion of realism to emphasize the surface of bent streets and the flatness of ramparts, dirt roads, and mosques with slender minarets.

Returning home, he painted his first pure abstract, *In the Style of Kairouan*, a flattened scape of minarets and mosaics in chockablock-and-lollipop shapes. Named for the city in northern Tunisia's inland desert, the painting appears in red, turquoise, yellow, olive green, orange, and blue to extrapolate variously the city's heat, its Mosque of the Three Doors, and its freshwater basins. The rectangles feel, to me, like prayer rooms, as distant from Mark Rothko's nuanced deep-purple and gray paintings, in a chapel in Houston, as possible, and yet as suggestive. Others soon named Klee's style "expressionism." His watercolors seem to intensify color. They make figures abstract and abstractions revelatory. Pyramids of spices and herbs, a cemetery of ramparts and hanging gardens. I find them utterly enchanting. In fact, they remind me of places I have never been.

2.

Nigerian artist Victor Ehikhamenor has spoken eloquently about the appropriation of art and artifacts from his homeland, spurred on by what he called "a fictionalizing of ideas" by artist Damien Hirst, who exhibited sculptures meant to be viewed as debris rescued from a shipwreck that never was. The shipwrecked "treasures," shown a few years ago at the Venice Biennale, depict pharaohs, sea beasts, carvings strangely resembling pop stars like Rihanna, and other kitsch items such as a barnacle-crusted Mickey Mouse. Also "revealed" by Hirst's "excavation" of the debris: a bronze head of Ife, a copy of a fourteenth-century Nigerian artwork. Representing a king of the Yoruba people, the original sculpture was dug up in 1938 and is a sacred object in Nigeria. Ehikhamenor called out Hirst's robbery: "I understand he is fictionalizing his ideas, but sleep should not be comparable to death, as my people would say." The Nigerian artist expressed his displeasure by another proverb—"My people have a saying: a woman whose child is bitten to death by a snake will not allow a wall gecko to come near another of her children."

3.

Compare Victor Ehikhamenor's condemnation of appropriation with literary critic Marjorie Perloff's assertion, in the *Boston Review*'s "Poetry on the Brink: Reinventing the Lyric," that, "Increasingly, 'the true voice of feeling' is the one you discover with an inspired, if sometimes accidental click." This idea roughly leads to borrowing a "true voice of feeling" for Hadara Bar-Nadav, by repurposing Paul Celan and Emily Dickinson lines for her elegy to her father, "Lullaby (with Exit Sign)," as she discusses in *The Volta*'s "The Post-Lyric Impulse: Appropriation and the Elegy." Without these geniuses, she reveals, she was unable to express her grief—"Dickinson's lines seemed to carry me, to hold me up and to hold the poem up"—a grief for which Perloff encourages other people's words, some intermediary "writing-through, grafting, mistranslating, and mashing," to reinvent a lyric "I" otherwise fraught with sentimentality and formulaic construction. Perloff describes the rubric for that "embarrassing bathos":

> The expression of a profound thought or small epiphany, usually based on a particular memory, designating the lyric speaker as a particularly sensitive person who really *feels* the pain, whether of our imperialist wars in the Middle East or of late capitalism or of some personal tragedy such as the death of a loved one.

In a review of Bar-Nadav's elegies in the *Kenyon Review*, Mike Puican sets one poem embedded with a Dickinson phrase parallel to the source:

> When I enter, the walls curl inward, cornering me. His unadorned form draped in a single white sheet. The seconds crush: *Grief is Tongueless*. Do not leave. Do not leave me alone. Broke of syntax. Quit of speech. The soul drifting, already in transit.

Dickinson's last stanza from "Grief is a Mouse":

> *Best Grief is Tongueless – before He'll tell*
> *Burn Him in the Public Square –*
> *His Ashes – will*
> *Possibly – if they refuse – How then know –*
> *Since a Rack couldn't coax a syllable – now*

Dickinson's phrase "Grief is Tongueless" is not simply another kind of writing from Bar-Nadav's, but another order. The anthropomorphizing of an abstraction, "Grief," as something deeply felt but hidden, is more insightful than Bar-Nadav's material description, "The walls curl inward," followed by a verbing of a noun, "cornering," which seems, in its pun, merely clever. Dickinson's act, because metaphysical and metaphorical, feels suggestive, where Bar-Nadav's physical room seems obvious, especially its "single white sheet."

Puican contends that, by embedding Dickinson, "This inclusion moves these poems beyond Bar-Nadav's overwhelming grief over the loss of her father and becomes a larger examination of how loss and other human vulnerabilities are dealt with through language. This, ultimately, is the book's central concern." The boost from Dickinson has certainly added a wild fragment to the fragments, but it hasn't really changed their function as shards, which remain discrete vortices rather than accumulate semantic knowledge.

The standing question is not whether writers ought to read and seek inspiration from other writers, but rather to what degree and toward what purpose ought the other texts be assimilated, appropriated, and integrated. Bar-Nadav has had a light touch with, and a reverence for, Emily Dickinson that is soulful, if not particularly artful, because Dickinson's phrases feel like they could be inserted anywhere, therefore nowhere.

The poet says of the wondrously strange art on her book's cover, Allison Schulnik's *Skipping Skeletons*, "It seems to insist on the vibrancy of the afterlife." The poems complement, without absorbing, the identity of the cover art, whereas Dickinson's life-breath feels grafted haphazardly over Bar-Nadav's prose poems. By contrast, her lineated poems have a beautiful, painful afterlife on their own. Dickinson becomes unnecessary, as in this fragment:

I slept with all four hooves

> *in the air or I slept like a snail*
> *in my broken shell.*

4.

Kenneth Goldsmith's much-maligned re-presentation of Michael Brown's autopsy report as a found poem illustrates the worst aspects of appropriation very starkly. At best, reframing the tragedy of an eighteen-year-old Black man murdered by a white police officer is a spectacle, a shock, perhaps even a compassionate act. But there seems no sorrow in it. Goldsmith's late conceptualism is reductionist hyper-realism. It lacks any spirit, whose self he has denounced as unstable, and therefore unreliable. The whole presumption that the removal of an emotional voice will provide a context for art is met squarely by other political and spiritual forces. Claudia Rankine quotes poet and politician Aimé Césaire in her epigraph to *Don't Let Me Be Lonely*, for example, on the structuring of social relations:

> And most of all beware, even in thought, of assuming the sterile attitude of the spectator, for life is not a spectacle, a sea of grief is not a proscenium, a man who wails is not a dancing bear.

When is appropriation cultural poaching?

5.

Charlie Chaplin's 1914 *Caught in the Rain*, the first film he both starred in and directed, erupts with conventional tramp drunk-gags and a frantic, final stretch of activity. Yet, Chaplin deploys these actions not as accessories, but rather as sacred artifacts by dignifying them with small touches and delayed reactions. These invent a nuanced character. The site of the vagabond—noble, eccentric, lonely, creative, and possibly death-defying—is a repository of history and wonder to which a mere stereotype cannot pay homage. As film critic Roger Ebert said of Chaplin's films, "They're not just a work. They're a place."

Also in the year 1914: *BLAST* printed its first issues, denouncing representation with experimental Vorticist art, a movement inspired by cubism and abstraction, then sharpened with the hard planes of industrial life. And, again in England that year, Yone Noguchi introduced lectures on the Japanese haiku. The point where inspiration slips into repurposing and appropriation is a point of contention, ethics, and drama.

6.

History in 1914 rolled out its massive war machine. In June, Franz Ferdinand, the Archduke of Austria, and Sophia, his wife, were murdered by a Serbian nationalist from a faction struggling to get the Austrians out of Bosnia and Herzegovina. The Russians, Britons, and French took the side of the Serbians. The Germans took the side of the Austrians. Europe dug itself in for four years of carnage to sort out the politics of it. Sixteen million soldiers and civilians died in this First World War in trenches, countrysides, and cities. For Paul Klee, born in Switzerland to a German father, it meant getting drafted as a thirty-six-year-old into the Reich.

Trained as an artist and deployed at an airfield, Klee's job was to stencil military figures onto planes. And when the young trainees crashed the planes, to record and photograph the aircraft, often downed with the tragic consequence of a mechanic caught in a propeller or a pilot impaled on a telephone pole. Klee reconfigured the aircrafts' fallen *flechettes* into his paintings in a desperate attempt at reclamation. These metal darts with sharp points were originally designed by some perverse mentality to be released over trenches to pierce a steel helmet or a human skull. The painter reconceived them as darting abstract arrows fraught with gaps, such that pigment reached only some angular zigzags, suggesting and exposing emptiness, brutality, and destruction.

Thus inspired by mechanical and commercial apparatus, and tormented by the atrocities of combat, he painted his way through part of the war, but with the rise of the Nazis, Klee, a Jew, was forced to flee to Switzerland. Using culture as a propaganda tool, the Germans condemned the paintings as degenerate.

7.

The experimental writer Marguerite Duras was born in Saigon in 1914 and spent her childhood in what was then called French Indochina. Her groundbreaking book, *The Lover*, a memoir written when she was seventy, explores an affair between a fifteen-year-old, poor white teenage girl and an older, wealthy Chinese businessman, set in the last years of French colonial rule. The prose itself is limpid. The businessman takes the child-prostitute to a secret Saigon apartment. The scandalous action unfolds as the girl undresses him:

> And she, slow, patient, draws him to her and starts to undress him. With her eyes shut. Slowly. He makes as if to help her. She tells him to keep still. Let me do it. She says she wants to do it. And she does. Undresses him.

The narrator slips between past and present and between first and third person, gesturing toward transgressions related to gender, race, and age. The work broke ground in the memoir but the memory, if it happened, gets told differently by Duras at other opportunities, until eventually, and perhaps melodramatically, the author announces:

The story of my life doesn't exist. Does not exist. There's never any centre to it. No path, no line. There are great spaces where you pretend there used to be someone, but it's not true, there was no one.

This makes me think, in a healthy, disorienting way, about freedom in art. It reminds me of Claudia Rankine's comment in an interview with Paul Legault, for the Academy of American Poets, about composition: "I don't feel any commitment to any external idea of the truth. I feel like the making of the thing is the truth, will make its own truth." Truth, variously interpreted as relative and absolute. Truth, variously interpreted as historical, imaginary, personal, shared, shifting, and liberating.

Marguerite Duras would become widely acclaimed for her meditation on war and love, *Hiroshima Mon Amour*, made into a film by Alain Resnais, in which an architect and actress engage in intimate conversation about memory and forgetting against the backdrop of a city destroyed by the atomic bomb. The work speaks in typical shorthand: "There's one thing I'm good at, and that's looking at the sea." It opens with a female voice recounting the ravaging of the city, the scarring and deforming of bodies and buildings, on August 6, 1945. The lovers are tortured by chaotic images of the present and past. The dialogue is intense and terrifying. Elle (French, "her") speaks from the trauma of a wartime liaison with a German officer in her French village. The Japanese architect, Lui (French, "him"), has a more immediate connection with the literal body of his native city crumbled. Aware their affair can't succeed, because she has family in France and he is married, she begins to call him "Hiroshima." He calls her, after her French village, "Nevers." Time as a nightmare, time obliterated. It is the opposite of sources and places as nourishing, fulfilling, and inspiring. Paradoxically, Duras's language has a searing beauty. At one point in *The Lover* someone says, "It's not that you have to achieve anything, it's that you have to get away from where you are."

8.

Although the painter Paul Klee was transformed by Tunisia, both he and Duras are familiar as Europeans. It's well known that Duras lived in Paris as an adult and worked in the Resistance during World War II, described in a fictionalized version in another of her disturbing books, *The War*, disturbing, that is, for at least the reason that she claims in a preface not to remember writing it. Because of the exoticizing of locales where they spent significant time, in Duras's case, during childhood and adolescence, and for Klee, during a few weeks' hiatus from his adult residence in Munich, some of their work raises issues of influence, co-option, and appropriation. Yet, those very places may have crystallized a style for them. Klee describes the inspiration as he drives around Tunis:

> Heavy sirocco wind, clouds, the extremely subtle definition of the colors. . . . To the rear, a big lake [Lac de Tunis], which is said to dry up in the summer. A slight feeling of desert, threatening. . . . We walked a little. First into a park with very peculiar plantings. Green-yellow-terracotta.

Klee also traveled outside Tunis to paint the cubical white houses and blue doorways in the central square of Sidi Bou Said, built on top of a cliff. Then, south to Hammamet:

> The city is magnificent . . . right by the sea, full of bends and sharp corners. Now and then I get a look at the ramparts! In the streets more women are to be seen than in Tunis. . . . The reeds and bushes provide a beautiful rhythm of patches. Superb gardens in the vicinity. Giant cactuses form walls. A path with cactuses. . . . Painted a good deal and sauntered around.

His is the fantasy of the visitor who has secured the money and set aside the time to experience leisure heightened by desire and ambition. It is the ultimate in tourist as traveler who appreciates, extrapolates, possesses, and is possessed:

> In the evening, through the streets. . . . An evening of colors as tender as they were clear. . . . I feel [my work] and it gives me confidence in myself without effort. Color possesses me. I don't have to pursue it. It will possess me always, I know it. That is the meaning of this happy hour: Color and I are one. I am a painter.

Does the outsider who visits such places inevitably mythologize them? Duras mashes memory, death, desire and colonialism:

On the sidewalk the crowd, going in all directions, slow or fast, forcing its way, mangy as stray dogs, blind as beggars, a Chinese crowd, I can still see it now in pictures of present prosperity, in the way they go along together without any sign of impatience, in the way they are alone in a crowd, without happiness, it seems, without sadness, without curiosity, going along without seeming to, without meaning to, just going this way rather than that, alone and in the crowd, never alone even by themselves, always alone even in the crowd.

Of necessity, the takeaway is subjective, reinforced by fictive figures of dogs and beggars, conjecture ("it seems"), obsessive repetition, run-ons, and paradox. It is either a gross generalization or astute commentary on poverty, laced with bigotry and lyricized with a formidable rhythmic tool kit. Duras is "reading" the signs and signature of the street as a newcomer or ingenue, a missed moment of liberation to reflect on oneself, one's melancholy, anxiety, or pleasure. Is she the cultural imperialist, the sociologist, the investigative journalist, the sentimentalist, the fetishist? As observer, her ethnography and mythology are at best no more than a dream or puzzle. At worst, a nightmare.

Descriptive language is a place where signs float freely. Poets build by reattaching them precariously and temporarily. What is a poet? One who would prefer to explore a center, whether it is empty or not, rather than indulge in a notoriously accepted system.

9.

In the United States, Margaret Caroline Anderson founded the *Little Review* in 1914 as part of Chicago's literary renaissance, publishing such experimental writers as Stevens, Stein, Williams, and Amy Lowell. Anderson soon met Jane Heap, an artist in the Chicago Arts and Crafts Movement, and they became lovers, working together on the *Review*. For a while they lived on a ranch in Muir Woods but settled in Greenwich Village. In "The Lesbian Partnership that Changed Literature," Emma Garman writes in the *Paris Review* of them:

> [Jane] was thirty-two, with cropped dark hair, a long straight nose, strong cheekbones, and a strikingly androgynous style. A typical outfit was

a men's frock coat, a high-necked shirt, and a tie. In winter, she added a Russian fur hat, and she always wore bright red lipstick. Anderson, three years her junior, had gone through a tomboy phase but was now exquisitely feminine, with a knack for projecting flawless chic despite never having any money. "Her profile was delicious," Janet Flanner recalled in a posthumous tribute for *The New Yorker*, "her hair blond and wavy, her laughter a soprano ripple, her gait undulating beneath her snug *tailleur*."

By avoiding traditional masculine and heterosexual appearances, especially with Jane Heap's innovative accompaniments to the proverbial men's suit—wearing lipstick and donning a fur hat—such butch-femme combinations rejected both visions of the dominant culture. Margaret, bored by the tomboy affect, revels in her *tailleur*, a snug, sophisticated jacket and skirt. Over a century later, a casual blazer, jeans, silk scarf, jewelry, and visible tattoos, a genderqueer's possible wardrobe, still prefers its radical and normative signs and signals mixed. What fun, appropriating, claiming, transgressing, and celebrating, like the queering of the color pink.

10.

The wanderer, or wandering Jew, as I understood the iconic traveler as a child, was on the move because of exodus or exile. I later learned the detail that the legendary figure perpetually walked the fields and deserts of the earth because he had the ignominious distinction of having taunted Jesus as he approached his death on the Cross, thereby consigning the shoemaker, such as he was, to his fate in an ironic twist.

An anonymous poet from around the tenth century who wrote "The Wanderer" didn't absorb the exiled life any better, soldiering on in despair after great happiness as one of his lordship's band when his comrades all died in battle. He mourns in grim, alliterative verse, "So heavy and heavier the hurt in heart / harrowing for the lost."

These tortured, nomadic presences slowly transmuted into a flâneur in my imagination, one who happily strolled and observed the world, as Baudelaire said:

> For the perfect *flâneur*, for the passionate spectator, it is an immense joy to set up house in the heart of the multitude, amid the ebb and flow of movement, in the midst of the fugitive and the infinite. To be away from home and yet to feel oneself everywhere at home; to see the world, to be at the centre of the world, and yet to remain hidden from the world—

Some among us always leave home for sustenance, inspiration, or change for an hour, a week, or a year, or perhaps, as some expatriates and immigrants prefer or require, simply hustle, as Paul Bowles put it in his autobiography's title, *Without Stopping*.

11.

Restless and peripatetic, writer and composer Paul Bowles was drawn to North Africa by its affordability, magic, and distance from New York. He lived in Tangier nearly half a century, so not exactly a tourist and no longer a rambler. Hisham Aidi, who knew Jane and Paul Bowles and later led walking tours of their neighborhood and favorite places, writes in the *New York Review of Books* of his radical change of heart about Bowles, in support of whom he had previously written:

> Although all the tropes of the Orientalist tradition—exotica, timelessness, barbarism—were there, Bowles should be spared the charge. Bowles, I argued, "places such an ironic twist on [Orientalist themes], essentially demonstrating their absurdity." He "is out to study Moroccans as a people, not as remnants of a primitive past."

Serious charges against Bowles began, as Aidi tells it, with accusations by Mohammed Choukri, Bowles's collaborator and protégé:

> Although [he] acknowledged Bowles's contributions to Tanjawi culture, not to mention his making possible the publication of Choukri's own story, [he] took the American to task for a nostalgia for the backward Morocco of an oppressive colonial era, and for packaging the stories he heard in cafés as the beginning of modern Moroccan literature. But the sentence that resounded above all was this: "Paul Bowles loves Morocco, but does not really like Moroccans."

While Aidi recognizes that Bowles defended the Berber population and wrote about the sultan's crackdown on Sufi practices, Bowles also exploited illiterate teenagers' stories and sexually abused them, as he himself details in personal letters. Back in the United States after visiting Algeria in his twenties, Bowles had already written composer Aaron Copeland about his sex life, "Where in this country can I have thirty-five or forty different people a week, and never risk seeing any of them again." The exploitation is criminal. As an old man, Bowles claims his sex life has always been "largely imaginary." Whether we think his bragging is bullshit or not, it neglects the question of whom might be dispossessed if we deform and repurpose the artifacts from our journey.

12.

If Paul Klee had not traveled to North Africa, he would never have changed the nature of his painting. Traveling south from Geneva, already opening to impressions, he wrote in a journal, "The little trees covered with red blossoms again, and the roofs became orange terra-cotta, enchanting, exactly my favourite shade of orange." By the time his boat crossed the Mediterranean, he felt the light "more glowing and rather darker—the evening is deep inside me forever."

We may imagine an early morning in which he observes a catch of orange roughy brought up glistening into a boat, or a night when he tastes the Tunisian hot chili pepper paste, harissa, which later transmogrify into a slab of orange oil paint. Forms, mystical hieroglyphs, and otherworldly creatures populate his compositions during and after the short sojourn. Suggestions of towers and palms combine with translucent color planes. Often the markings seem communal shapes from the unconscious, watery and shadowy. In calling it "Tunisia," do we co-opt someone's center, sunrise, twisted lane, and clifftop village? What am I doing here?

More to the point, I ask myself after three decades, why ever think the Tohono O'odham people's desert I inhabit becomes "mine," especially when the double entendre, "mine," as in, "extract and remove," haunts the query? For the record, Arizona mines most of this country's copper, scaring the fragile land and polluting its air and water. So the haunting is real and local. In what way is the area's endangered pygmy owl ever available to a writer for examination and transformation? This fierce, and fiercely monogamous, creature, with its piercing golden stare and tiny body in brown-sepia, decamps from the mesquite woods to my front lantern to hoot and roost, rather than settle into its more common lodging in a saguaro cactus hole. It has a unique language and vibration. Much might be inferred, depicted, or mythologized. Shall I make it my "subject," knowing that word's history of subjugation? Meanwhile, less than six inches high, the owl hides in a discrete corner outside the bedroom window to breed. Under the Endangered Species Act, to kill, injure, or interfere with the owl is to commit a "take," a Federal crime.

"To interfere," from Old French s'entreferir, "to strike each other," implicates artists *physically* with the substance of their attention. If it is the poet's calling to describe, imagine, and fortify the universe of old remnants and ideas with new energy, one must also consider the limits of empathy on borrowed sources.

What more is a poet? Someone rustling between the fixed and the mutable, beyond origin or destination. Osip Mandelstam is barely in his twenties in 1914, having recently converted because the University of Saint Petersburg excluded Jews. He is already writing "The Morning of Acmeism," morning as in "beginning," but also "freshness," a credo in which "beauty is not the whim of a semi-god, it is the relentless eye of a simple carpenter." As his part of the planet goes to war, he describes the poet as a citizen-worker of the world. He has just published the poems of his first book, *Stone*, which speaks, through a translation by Merwin and Clarence Brown, from this broad vantage:

And over the evening forest
the bronze moon climbs to its place.
Why has the music stopped?
Why is there such silence?

Mandelstam voiced perhaps the ultimate humility: "To love the existence of the object more than the object itself, and existence more than oneself." He later would write of a poet's moral heritage in referring to Dante's "grandiose music of trustfulness, of trust, in the nuances—delicate as an alpine rainbow—of probability and conviction."

What is there in the twenty-first century for an artist to believe in? Our imagination courses through everything around us, until life itself is a kaleidoscopic study from morning through darkness to morning. As one opens, one's own light obfuscates or complements the world. When I had no opportunity or means, I used to think that a house by the sea was an honorable goal in life. I felt that I would hurt no one by moving closer to nature. But there is something elegant about the gravitational force of the universe, which pulls us toward one another slowly, but truly. A poet processes the substance of things in words with ancient origins like ours, elements as natural as oils, olives, and nuts, as a small part of an inexorable movement toward interdependency and connectivity, what some call illumination. We stand in our own shadow, in the shadow of our mentors, and those now at work.

Our role is to be vulnerable to the poem, which is an action and a contemplation. Mandelstam explains the authority of a passage from his maestro: "There exists no power on earth which could hasten the movement of honey from a tilted glass jar."